P9-DEA-072

THE LIFE@WORK BOOK

by

The Editors of the *The Life@Work Journal*

WORD PUBLISHING

NASHVILLE

A Thomas Nelson Company

To Grant and Carol Nelson. When *The Life@Work Journal*
was just an idea   no staff, no journal, no subscribers,
no market momentum, just an idea   you guys joined up.
Your investment launched *The Life@Work Journal* into existence.
Thanks from everyone all over the world who has been
or ever will be touched by *The Life@Work Journal.*

■ ■ ■

THE LIFE@WORK BOOK

Copyright ' 2000 Cornerstone Companies

Published by Word Publishing, a unit of Thomas Nelson, Inc., P.O. Box 141000, Nashville, Tennessee 37214. No
portion of this book may be reproduced, stored in a retrieval system, or transmitted in any form or by any
means electronic, mechanical, photocopy, recording, or other except for brief quotations in printed reviews,
without the prior permission of the publisher.

ISBN 0-8499-4243-8

Printed in the United States of America
00 01 02 03 04 05 PHX 6 5 4 3 2 1

Contents

99750

Part Four —Taking the Lead

Part Five — The Future

Introduction:
The Flames of a Revolution

LAURA NASH, AUTHOR OF *Believers in Business*, tells a story that very well could have been told by any of the writers in this volume. She was traveling by plane in the early 1990s when the person seated next to her asked what she was working on. When she said she was writing a book on CEOs who were followers of Christ, she got *the look*. "I might as well say I'm working on ancient forms of sexual perversion," Nash wrote, "to judge from the curious mix of contempt and fascination with which the information is usually greeted."

If that conversation were repeated today, it might elicit a different response. Spirituality in the workplace has gone mainstream. Late in 1998, *USA Today* made the claim that, "In the 21st century, more religious leaders will be found in the corporation than in the conventional church." (Nov. 17, 1998) A year later, *Business Week* ran a cover story on spirituality and work, noting that "a spiritual revival is sweeping across Corporate America" and "gone is the old taboo against talking about God at work." (Nov. 1, 1999)

What began as isolated pockets of interest about how faith and work intersect quickly is turning into a widespread phenomenon. A cultural trend is becoming a cultural movement. Newspapers report it, magazines feature it, and seminars explain it. When we launched *The Life@Work Journal* in 1998, books on this category were trickling off the presses. Now publishers send us 15 to 20 new titles each month.

There exists a deep hunger for an integrated existence that somehow brings together all the different parts of life. Instead of considering work separate from church, separate from hobbies, separate from family, folks feel an urgent need to consolidate all of life's elements into some kind of whole. From a demographic perspective, the Builder generation is more tolerant of separation between different parts of life than is the Boomer generation. That same trend holds true between the Baby Boomers and Generation X. Baby Boomers pushed the envelope by loosening up the dress code for Fridays and switching careers at midlife to pursue something of greater significance in their second half. The Next

Generation asks the completely logical question: "Why only dress comfortably one day a week?" And they prefer that every work project in which they are involved yield both success *and* significance. Why wait until midlife for the meaningful stuff to start?

The current hunger for integration between work and faith is a rare instance of a cultural appetite bonding with a Biblical mandate. From the earliest pages of Genesis, the Scriptures affirm the importance of work, as well as the inextricable link between the labor we are called to individually and a life of vibrant faith. Jesus provides a road map that takes secular society precisely where it says it wants to go—toward a life more whole.

Unfortunately, many of the spiritual answers being given to work questions do not reflect a Christ-centered view of the world. Unlike the arena of marriage and family, in which the majority of the content in a typical bookstore might come from a Biblical perspective, spirituality and work is dominated by a New Age agenda, or similar kinds of thought. With rare exception, followers of Christ have been late to pull a chair up to the conference table and engage in the discussion.

This volume is an attempt to make available again—to bring back to the table—some of the best thinking on the integration of work and faith in Jesus from writers who engaged in the discussion before there was a cultural trend,

much less a cultural movement. In many respects, the authors represented in this book were alone in the wilderness shouting at the trees. They had a wonderful message, but lacked an eager audience. They had the Biblical mandate, but the culture lacked a spiritual hunger. The idea behind putting together a "best of" book was to give readers a glimpse of these foundational works.

We settled on fourteen books that were written over the past thirty years. Most still are in print; some are not. We did not include a selection from every great book on this category, nor did we include something from every relevant writer. What we did was attempt to present some of the best thinking in the category of faith and work in a way that gives you, the reader, a solid basis for integrating your faith and your work. This is not an end-all compilation on this category; it is merely the beginning.

WORK IN PERSPECTIVE

Some historical perspective is in order before we introduce you to the works represented in this volume. Although the concept of integration might be revolutionary stuff for our time, it is not a new idea. Following the New Testament Era, during which integration between work and faith was taken for granted and practiced well, four overarching historical periods saw major shifts toward the separation between work and the other parts of life and back again toward wholeness. We have named them as follows: Separation: the sacred/secular split (300 to 1517); Reformation: the sacred/secular healing (1517 to 1730); Fragmentation: the Industrial Revolution (1730 to 1980s); and Integration (1980s to present).

From roughly 300 to 1517 A.D., the church made a distinction—subtly at first and then with real force—between the secular and the sacred. Specifically, all church-related professions were deemed sacred and everything else was secular. The priority and hierarchy was obvious: Anything secular was second-class. The important and God-ordained work was reserved for those associated directly with the church. The bad news was that the church took apart what Scripture clearly taught was to be together.

The good news is that the church put the sacred and the secular back together in the second historical period—from around 1517 to 1730. The Reformation had as one of its central tenets that all work was sacred. If a person was engaged in a career assigned by God's call, then that work—whether plumbing work or pastoral work—had eternal significance. That fresh—and Biblical—thinking brought tremendous dignity to the majority of men and women who worked outside the boundaries of what had been deemed "sacred."

Toward the middle of the eighteenth century, culture began to fragment what the church had reunited during The Reformation. The Industrial Revolution was predicated—at least partly—on the assumption that in order for work to be efficient it had to be divided. Up to that point, most individuals were involved in the entire process of their work tasks. Blacksmiths, for example, did everything from designing an implement, heating and shaping the metal, and selling the product.

Adam Smith contended in *The Wealth of Nations*, published in 1776, that such a comprehensive approach to work did not allow laborers to concentrate on specific tasks and, thus, to use their time most effectively. He suggested that the work process be segmented so that a worker could specialize in a specific task, thus yielding both speed and product uniformity. The resulting assembly line technology revolutionized how most goods were manufactured and services delivered. But it also fragmented work processes to such an extent that to this day workers often are unaware of what else takes place in producing a good or service beyond their own small part.

While Smith's ideas were in many ways brilliant, even he saw the inherent dangers of industrialization—greed, violence, the loss of an individual's value as something more than a unit of production. Yet for the most part, the downside to such fragmentation wasn't recognized until the mid 1980s when total quality management gained popularity throughout the workforce. Total quality is impossible if those involved in a process do not have input into its creation, and it is very difficult to have adequate input without knowing what happens upstream and downstream to the task being evaluated. So, slowly at first and then with accelerated velocity, work processes that had been fragmented began to come back together.

The integration of the distinct parts of work also is fueled by the cultural trends in which the Boomers, and especially the Gen-Xers, are toppling barriers between work and other parts of life, as well as between the different segments of work life. The resulting inclination toward integration is perhaps as significant as the drift toward fragmentation at the inauguration of the Industrial Revolution.

For the first time since the Reformation, followers of Christ are starting to embrace the approach to work theology outlined concisely in the early 1970s by Bill Hybels in *Christians in the Marketplace*: "True believers cannot compartmentalize their lives. They cannot go to church and Bible studies and other 'Christian activities' wearing sanctified masks of godliness, and then trade them for the more comfortable masks of worldliness as they enter the marketplace. . . . When the true Christian enters the marketplace, Christ enters with him, and together they must leave their mark of holiness."

SEARCHING FOR THAT MARK

The Life@Work Co. was launched as part of the movement that is turning the idea of segmentation on its head. This movement, dare we say, is a revolution of God's call for living an integrated life according to His plan. It is that revolution that brought the editors of this book together, each traveling vastly different roads that ended up intersecting in pursuit of a common destination.

Addington, Graves, and Womack are cofounders of The Life@Work Co. Griffith is the Chief Operating Officer. Caldwell is the executive editor of *The Life@Work Journal*. When the cover says this book was compiled by the "Life@Work editors," it is referring to this team.

Collectively, we have cleaned houses, driven tractor trailers, delivered waterbeds, pushed creative processes, edited newspapers, consulted, led various organizations, and taught at universities.

Addington spent most of his formative years in Hong Kong, where, among other things, he painted some of the interior walls in the missionary hospital his father helped found. He also drove an 18-wheeler while in college, identifying himself on the CB radio as "the bishop."

Graves worked a variety of odd jobs to pay his way through college and seminary—everything from working in a feed mill to refereeing football games to delivering waterbeds. In the early 1990s,

Graves and Addington founded a consulting company that focuses on "blending Biblical wisdom and business excellence." Using Scripture as their guide, they began helping business leaders—in companies of all shapes and sizes—deal with such complex issues as organizational change.

Womack cleaned houses, worked as a bank teller, made pasta in an Italian restaurant, and drew editorial cartoons for the local newspaper during college, then rose through the management ranks of DaySpring Greeting Cards before helping cofound The Life@Work Co.

Griffith, who once owned a fishing business in Florida, was a staff director for a large but still growing church when he caught the vision for applying his leadership skills in a business environment.

Caldwell had worked in the newspaper industry his entire life. Not long after submitting his life to Jesus, he felt the call to do more writing that dealt with faith. At the time, he thought it meant freelancing for "Christian" magazines. Instead, it meant helping to launch a magazine for followers of Christ in the marketplace.

This is the team that selected the works that make up this book. But we aren't pioneers of the movement. Not for the ages. And not even for our generation.

Part of what brought our team together was the fact that there were others before us leading the way. They might have felt at times as if they were shouting at nothing but the trees, but it simply took time for those who heard their message to find their way together. That's how a movement starts—with independent fires that somehow united into something far bigger than the sparks that created them.

As we looked back at fourteen sparks, we focused our attention on five areas that are relevant to the integration of work and faith: the foundations, the hurdles, the tools, the leaders, and the future. By the conclusion we ought to agree not only that our work matters to God, as authors Doug Sherman and Bill Hendricks point out, but also that God matters to our work.

Part One draws on the works of Hybels, Sherman and Hendricks, and Michael Novak to provide the essential building blocks for understanding God's view of work and how we should respond to that view.

Part Two looks at some of the hurdles followers of Christ face when attempting to integrate their faith and their work. Chapters from books by Os Guinness, Charles Colson and Jack Eckerd, and Laura Nash combine theory, practical experience, and solid research to present different looks at the struggles of taking a Biblical approach to work.

Part Three examines some practical solutions to living an integrated life. Larry Burkett explains how to create and run a Biblically based business. William Pollard makes a case for being a proactive, lifelong learner. And Charles Swindoll shows how vision leads to productivity.

Part Four focuses on leadership and includes chapters from Laura Beth Jones, Max De Pree, and John Maxwell. And Part Five provides some guidance for the future from Bob Buford and the late Bob Briner.

It's a pretty diverse cast of writers. Some come from academic backgrounds, some from ministry backgrounds, some from business backgrounds, and some from a combination of all three. They represent an assortment of theological perspectives. And their writing styles are as diverse as the food offerings at a company picnic.

As with any "best of" book, you will relate to some authors and some offerings more than others. Some like chicken; some spaghetti. But we feel each selection has something valuable that will start you on the path of exploring the integration of faith and work. We welcome you to this banqueting table. Enjoy the meal.

PART ONE
The Foundations

Bill Hybels has a reputation for living and working ahead of the curve. In the 1970s, as a recent college graduate helping to lead a college ministry, Hybels became one of the pioneers of a national movement toward innovation and creativity in the church.

As a founding pastor of Willow Creek Community Church in suburban Chicago, he helped redefine "church" and "ministry" for an entire generation, especially those who were seeking a relationship with God. At the heart of this innovation was a desire to meet people where they were—spiritually, intellectually, and physically.

It should come as no surprise that Hybels wrote one of the first major works on the category of faith and work. *Christians in the Marketplace*, published in 1982, answered some foundational questions about what God has to say about work.

In the first chapter of the book, Hybels debunks old-school thinking that work is merely the byproduct of the curse (Gen. 3:17–19), a symptom of the disease of inherently evil hearts.

Instead, Hybels promotes a more sound theology of work. In "Human Labor: Necessary Evil, or God's Design?" Hybels argues that work is a good institution made by God that comes to us as both a privilege and a mandate.

Many people seem to misunderstand foundational truth. Too often, we see work as a curse—something brought on because of the fall. Our goal in life is to stop working.

Hybels shows that Scripture paints a different picture. Work is something God created and something God participates in. It is something mankind did before the fall and something mankind will do when Christ's Kingdom is fully restored. Work might not always be easy, but it's certainly not evil. It is part of God's plan.

"Labor was not a punishment; neither was it an afterthought," Hybels writes. *"Labor was the design."*

Hybels also introduces the concept that truths learned in the intersection of work and faith are transcendent. Lessons learned in the crucible of the marketplace are frequently transferable to other parts of life, even our spiritual lives.

"What we learn in the marketplace also spills over into our spiritual lives," he writes.

In our labor, there is value—value in responsibility, value in accomplishment, and value in dignity. Diligent labor produces the reward of dignity. And dignity is available to *everyone*. So what's the rush to retire?

1 "Human Labor: Necessary Evil or God's Design"

from *Christians in the Marketplace* by Bill Hybels

"I WANT TO BUY a new car, pay off my house, quit my job, and *never work again!*" So goes the typical response of a recent lottery winner or recipient of a generous inheritance. *I'm never going to work again! I can rid myself of the curse of mankind! I'll be free!* I wonder how many people would like to echo those words and cast off the chains of labor.

Work seems to have risen to the status of the number one necessary evil in this country. The average person endures the weekly grind only by relishing the anticipation of the workless weekend; and nearly everyone plans for an early retirement. Even Christians share this view. They believe that labor came about by default, rather than by the design of God. They envision God screaming at Adam and Eve in relentless anger: "You despicable sinners. There's only one thing horrible enough to be a fitting punishment for your disobedience. You shall work! Work! Work!" The picture of human labor is painted with sadistic, vengeful strokes.

Is that how God would have us view labor—as the dreadful punishment due fallen man? Genesis 1 paints the first picture of labor. We read that "God created . . . and God was moving . . . and God separated . . . and God called . . . and God made . . . and God gathered . . . and God placed . . . and God blessed." Step by step, day by day, God labored over Creation. The labor was not His curse, His punishment. It was His choice. He willfully, voluntarily, and joyfully brought this world into existence, and when He finished and studied His Creation He said, "Yes, this is *very good.*" The result of His skillful work brought Him joy and a tremendous sense of accomplishment.

The next biblical picture of labor is in Genesis 2, where God told Adam to cultivate and care for the Garden of Eden. Adam had not yet sinned, so surely there could be no vengeance in this command. On the contrary, God was saying, "Adam, I love you. I've already given you time, and now I choose to give you something precious and worthwhile to do with your time. Enjoy the beauty of My Creation and help Me preserve it." Adam didn't complain. He didn't ask for a negotiation table, for greater benefits, for higher *pay*. Apparently he accepted the responsibility joyfully as a meaningful assignment from God.

Labor was not a punishment; neither was it an afterthought. *Labor was the design*. It was God's way of filling man's days with pleasant, meaningful activity. Unfortunately, after man's fall into rebellion and sin, the nature of labor was somewhat altered. No longer did the ground yield its fruit willingly; instead, it produced with reluctance, thorns and thistles complicating the task. Sweat and toil and struggle and frustration claimed their place in the picture as the need for labor increased. In spite of this twisting by sin, however, the basic value of human labor remains unchanged. Labor still richly rewards those who accept its yoke and still retains those elements which mark it as God's design for us. Associated with it are invaluable benefits which God willingly directs into our lives as a reward for diligent work.

THE DIGNITY OF WORK

Have you ever watched a skilled worker in the midst of his labors and noticed the gleam that sparkled in his eyes as he watched the fruit of his efforts slowly ripen and then mature? Have you ever experienced the self-respect, the self-confidence, and the healthy independence that comes when you tackle a difficult task for which you have carefully and patiently prepared?

If you have, then you've seen and experienced the dignity of diligent labor.

Not long ago my wife and I hired a professional decorator to hang wallpaper in our house. Always before we had hung wallpaper ourselves, but our last project had taught us a vital lesson. If we wanted to do it right and if we wanted to preserve our marriage, we had to hire a pro. In our first house we spent the better part of a weekend in a five-foot by five-foot bathroom, trying to get the wallpaper to stay on the walls. We weren't asking for anything fancy. We just wanted it to stick. We fought, we complained, we climbed all over each other trying to cut the paper and spread the paste. Finally we got the paper on the walls and breathed a sigh of relief, until we noticed the paper shrinking and the lumps rising. We had to pull it down and start again. We spent most of the weekend trying to wallpaper that little bathroom, and the rest of it trying to salvage our marriage. Never again would we try that!

What a treat it was to watch a skilled craftsman. He didn't have to read the directions on the back of the rolls. He didn't have to use a tape measure to check every single move he made. He didn't pour water and paste all over the bathroom floor. He didn't pray as he approached the corner of the medicine cabinet (as I had been compelled to do!). He didn't even buy two extra rolls of paper to compensate for mistakes. He worked quickly and confidently and joyfully, and completed what I considered a two-day job in just a few hours.

I was amazed. "How did you do that?" I inquired. "Did God give you a divine endowment? A special gift? What's your secret?" He smiled innocently and explained. "Practice, that's all. Just practice."

What was he saying in that simple response? He was saying that he had labored diligently over the years to perfect his God-given ability. He had made mistakes, of course, but he had recovered from them, and he had learned to think clearly and organize carefully and execute skillfully. Gradually he had developed confidence in his ability to use what God had given him to accomplish his God-given goal. In short, he had experienced dignity. Diligent labor produces dignity in the man or woman who is willing to commit himself or herself to it.

God knew what dignity would do for a man or woman, and in His grace He designed labor, whether it be in the home or in the marketplace, as a means of helping people develop dignity. Naturally, some people, through no fault of their own, are unable to work. For them God undoubtedly provides another means of developing dignity. But to most people meaningful labor is a viable option, and to them I pose this question: Can people who deliberately refuse to labor develop dignity?

To the generation which preceded mine, there is no need to ask this question. Not only was the value of human labor acknowledged, but it was often so heavily emphasized that it produced the destructive imbalance of workaholism. My generation has recognized the danger of this imbalance, but for many the pendulum has swung too far. Today it is not uncommon for an individual to openly attempt to finagle his way through life without working, with little thought given to the responsibilities of the future. Can this person develop dignity? I think not. Dignity does not float down from heaven; it cannot be purchased nor manufactured. It is a reward reserved for those who labor with diligence.

I've heard it said—and probably some of you reading this book would agree—that dignity is available to a higher degree to those in white-collar jobs who can afford the big homes and fancy cars and who gain the recognition of others. But I beg heartily to differ with this assumption. *Dignity is available to every person in every legitimate, worthwhile profession.*

The farmer who plows the straight furrow, the accountant whose books balance, the truckdriver who backs his 40-foot trailer into a narrow loading dock, the teacher who delivers a well-prepared lesson, the carpenter who keeps the building square, the executive who reads the market accurately, the factory worker who labors with speed and accuracy, the secretary who types the pages perfectly, the student who masters a foreign language, the athlete who plays the game aggressively, the mother who tends the children faithfully, the minister who prepares his sermon and preaches it powerfully—all these people can experience dignity as they commit themselves to their labors.

The writer of the Book of Proverbs says, "Do you see a man skilled in his work? He will stand before kings; he will not stand before obscure men" (22:29). Obviously this doesn't mean that every individual who is skilled in his work will be called to the White House. It does mean, however, that there is a sense of royalty, a sense of honor, associated with diligent labor. Meeting the President face-to-face is not the point. Human dignity is the point. And God has made it available to all who will work.

RESPONSIBILITY

Labor helps us develop not only dignity, but also a sense of responsibility. In Proverbs 26:13-14 we read, "The sluggard says, 'There is a lion in the road! A lion is in the open square!' Like the door turns on its hinges, so does the sluggard on his bed." The sluggard, the loafer, the person unwilling to commit himself to diligent labor says, "There's a lion on the street." *I cannot go there. I might get hurt. I might be uncomfortable. I might not like it.* He uses every excuse he can conceive to stay away from his labors, and gradually develops a lazy, irresponsible attitude. "As the door

turns on its hinges, so does the sluggard on his bed." Unwilling to accept his responsibilities, he turns his back on them, and eventually becomes oblivious to them.

Though most of us learn a certain level of responsibility in the nuclear family and also in school, nowhere do we learn it to the degree that we learn it in the marketplace. Job descriptions, defined duties, performance expectations, ultimatums—they all exert their positive pressure on us. Either we meet the requirements or we lose the job. In this way, the marketplace forces us to accept the challenge of responsible adulthood.

The marketplace teaches us responsibility in two specific areas. The first area is our personal schedules. My own experience illustrates this. During the summers of my high school years, I never had a set curfew. My father allowed me to stay out as late as I chose, provided I was able to be at work on time the next morning. Now, that idea sounded just great to a 16-year-old kid, but there was more wisdom and guidance provided in that demand than I at first realized. You see, each morning I had to begin loading the trucks at our family-owned produce warehouse at 6 A.M., and I had to work until 5 P.M. Every day. There were no exceptions. How long do you think it took me to learn that I couldn't do a whole day's work on a half night's sleep? Two days. After two days of near insanity, I made the decision. *I will be in bed early every night.* I didn't care what my friends did or what they thought of me. *I will be in bed early, because I must be at work at 6.*

How thankful I am that I learned that lesson early. Diligent labor has provided me with a clear understanding of the needs of my personal schedule. I know that if I have a message to give that requires an unusual amount of study, or if I have traveling or outside speaking engagements to consider, I must adjust my schedule accordingly. I will need to eliminate something else in order to fulfill the requirements of my job. I must properly care for myself physically and emotionally, so that I can be at work on time and produce an honest day's work.

Those on staff at my church know how I feel about promptness. We begin our day at the office at 9:00, not 9:02, or even 9:01. Am I a tyrant? No. I simply believe that I can serve those under my supervision best by teaching them responsibility with regard to their schedules. I do not believe I am hurting them, but rather helping them to develop a habit and a consciousness that will be of value to them for as long as they live. If I can help them learn responsibility with respect to their work schedules, I can then encourage them to be responsible with their time as it relates to their health, their marriages, their ministries, their personal devotions in the morning, etc. My goal, therefore, is not just to get them to work on time. but to teach them a sound principle for living.

Human labor, then, teaches us responsibility in terms of our schedule. It also teaches responsibility with respect to our performance. The words of the marketplace ring loud and clear, "You do your job well, or we will find someone else who will." It's that simple. Though it sounds cold and ruthless, such expectations can be highly motivational to the men and women who willingly accept the challenges of their jobs. In life there are certain things we love to do, and other things we hate to do. So it is in the marketplace. In every job assignment there are certain tasks we pursue with pleasure, and others we abhor. The marketplace says, "You will do them both, or you will do nothing." That, I contend, can be good. It can provide just the challenge and discipline we need.

Once again consider my high school work experience.* Each summer, in addition to our responsibilities at the produce warehouse, my brother and I also had to spend some time working on a farm owned by the company. In late May we began plowing, disking, and dragging the fields, preparing them for planting. In all

---

*Though I don't want to spend too much time talking about myself, I do believe God allowed me to have these experiences so that I could learn personally the lesson of the secular marketplace and share them with others. Throughout this book, any references to myself and my experiences are used only to aid in clarifying a given point.

seriousness, this job was sheer delight. We took off our shirts, made ourselves comfortable on the tractor seats, and thoroughly enjoyed the sunshine and fresh air. It was a welcome change from the months of winter and classrooms and books.

Unfortunately, in early August, when it was hot and humid and the pleasure of being out in the sun had begun to fade, we had to face a different job which we both dreaded. We had to spray the onion fields with a certain chemical which caused the pupils of our eyes to dilate. Needless to say, pupil dilation causes tremendous pain when you're outside on a bright, sunny day. If we tried to pinch our eyes shut to avoid exposure to the light, we ran over rows of onions, destroying the crop. If we wore sunglasses, the dust and tears combined to cover the glasses with so much grime that again we couldn't see. There was no alternative but to bear the pain and do the best we could.

To this day I claim that was a beneficial experience for us. The farm, our marketplace, taught us that there were certain things we had to do whether we enjoyed them or not. That is the lesson of the marketplace.

Why, you might ask, is that lesson so valuable? Because in all of life we must learn to take the bad with the good. There are times when my relationship with my wife is the source of untold pleasure, when it provides all I need of support and encouragement and human companion-ship. At other times it is the source of intense frustration and difficulty, even pain. Here then, I can apply the lesson of the marketplace. We don't quit just because times are tough. We accept the bad with the good.

What we learn in the marketplace also spills over into our spiritual lives. At times, putting together messages for my congregation is pure bliss and excitement. At other times, I page through the Bible and can glean nothing from its pages. The experience is drudgery, dry, empty; but still I must stand before an entire church and give a message. I have no choice but to keep working and working and working, until I can discern God's message for the people. Do these times cause me to question my place in the ministry? Do they make me wonder if I am actually walking with the Lord? No, they just remind me again that I must consciously and consistently persevere through times of difficulty.

Remember the sluggard and learn from his ways. Don't create excuses to keep yourself from your labors. Allow labor to teach you responsibility.

ACCOMPLISHMENT

In the marketplace we learn dignity, we learn responsibility, and finally, we learn to enjoy a sense of accomplishment. After creating our world, God acknowledged that it was "very good" (Gen. 1:31). He expressed and recorded for all time His satisfaction with the world which He had created. It appears to me that He had the emotional vulnerability to tell everyone who reads His Book that the labor of His hands brought Him tremendous pleasure. It was beautiful. It was the product of His love. *It was good.*

Nothing builds self-esteem and self-confidence like accomplishment. Though I maintain some points of contention with the positive thinkers of our day, in this regard I agree with them fully. Success breeds success. When a labor experience results in accomplishment, it provides motivation for the next assignment. Having toiled and cried and sacrificed to see a task through to completion, the laborer experiences the joy of a job well done, and that moves him to begin the cycle again. His success, his sense of accomplishment, prods him back to his labors.

Many claim that because sin has infiltrated this world, feelings of satisfaction and fulfillment are rare and hard to attain. The marketplace, however, affords us regular opportunities to launch and labor over and complete various tasks. As each of these tasks is completed, there is that brief but blessed moment that brings the payoff. Think of the salesman who finally signs the dotted line for the big sale, the student who types the last page of the term paper, the mother who tucks the last child in bed, the doctor who finds the cure, the farmer who finishes the field, the musician who completes the encore, the maintenance worker who turns off the vacuum, the teacher who says, "Class dismissed!" the mason who lays the last brick. To these people, labor graciously affords many moments of accomplishment that can be savored for a lifetime.

In closing this chapter, I quote the great Apostle Paul, who labored joyfully in his ministry and in the secular marketplace as well. "I have fought the good fight, I have finished the course, I have kept the faith; in the future there is laid up for me the crown of righteousness, which the Lord, the righteous Judge, will award to me on that day; and not only to me, but also to all who have loved His appearing" (2 Tim 4:7-8). Who can love the appearing of the Lord but those who have labored well for Him? Whether in the marketplace or in the ministry, we can labor diligently as unto the Lord, and receive the crown of righteousness, His seal of approval.

Turning again to Scripture, we read The ultimate words of accomplishment, which Jesus uttered from the cross. "It is finished!" (John 19:30). Hanging naked, in agony suspended between heaven and earth, the holy Son of God performed the supreme labor of love. His work in paying for our sins, in securing our eternal redemption, and in opening for us the very doors of life itself, was completed. Surely no greater pain could have been experienced by man, and yet surely no greater joy. His job was finished. Forever. For you and me.

from the editors of *The Life@Work Journal*

. . .

In many ways, Bill Hendricks and Doug Sherman were prophets when they wrote *Your Work Matters to God*. They put their fingers on the pages of Scripture and articulated truths that would not begin to be acknowledged in a significant way in our culture for at least another decade. Written in 1987, the book was ahead of its time, but it completely aligns with the felt needs of today's culture.

This probably comes as no shock to its authors. In 1974, they point out in the preface, Seward Hiltner wrote that "Christianity needs a theology of work—and quickly." This book was born out of that sense of urgency.

The authors were representational of the movement they helped to launch. Both completed degrees from Dallas Theological Seminary, but neither saw traditional ministry as their calling. They took what they had learned, and what they continued to study, about God's Word and began applying it in the marketplace. In doing so, they were struck by the urgent need for followers of Jesus to make a more clear and real connection between faith and work.

In this chapter, Sherman and Hendricks (through the narrative of Sherman) push the idea that our work should be God's work, and when it isn't, we are out of line.

"But I would like to suggest that as humans, we need to view our work as His work. We need to do it His way. And we need to trust Him for His results," writes Sherman.

Because our work is God's work, the authors argue, it is not insignificant. On the contrary, Sherman and Hendricks build the case that work was designed by God to satisfy a rich multitude of life needs in addition to economic necessity.

The chapter constructs handles for understanding how God's plan for work intersects with our motives and our work style. The chapter apexes with a discussion of the results of making God's work our work and how those results address many needs, from the pragmatic to the immaterial (boredom, careerism).

This chapter is a top-line summary of what it means to work for God as a child of God versus working for one's self as a child of God. It is about doing His work, His way, and achieving His results. By seeing our work as an extension of God's work, the authors point out, we can find real dignity in doing our work the way God wants it done.

2 Working for God— His Work, His Way, His Results

from *Your Work Matters to God*
by Doug Sherman and William Hendricks

ANYONE WHO HAS BEEN in the service is familiar with the old cliché: There's the right way, the wrong way, and the Navy way!

That pretty much sums up life in any mammoth institution. If you're a rank-and-file member, you're not paid to think—just do your job.

Things were not much different in the Air Force. From day one, they helped me understand that the system did not exist to serve me; rather, I was there to serve the system. As you can well imagine, this came as something of a shock to me as a seventeen-year-old cadet!

That's why I chuckle sometimes at the popular conception of fighter jocks. Novels, TV, and films convey the idea that the defense of our country rests on twenty-two-year-old kids cowboying across the skies in screaming hunks of techno-exotica fueled by jet-powered libido.

I assure you life in the cockpit is much more disciplined. Much more!

We served an extremely elaborate code of instructions, regulations, and protocol designed to ensure efficiency, safety, order, and, as much as anything, respect.

The tolerance for violating this code was as thin as a discharge order.

In short, we were commissioned to do the Air Force's work, the Air Force's way. Why? In order to achieve the Air Force's results. That's why we called our flights "missions." They always had a purpose behind them. We were never simply joy-riding across the skies.

Now this way of life is somewhat similar to the way our work relates to God. I stress "somewhat" because God is not a drill sergeant barking orders from heaven. Nor is His tolerance for our failures so slight.

But I would like to suggest that as humans, we need to view our work as *His work*. We need to do it *His* way. And we need to trust Him for *His results*. Let's unpack these principles.

HIS WORK: OUR MOTIVES

God is a Worker and has created you in His image to be His coworker. Consequently, your work is an extension of God's work. Furthermore, your work is a means whereby you can fulfill His Great

Commandments: to love Him, to love other people, and to love yourself. So as a Christian, you are to go to work for the same reason you go to church: to worship and serve Christ. Though you obey human bosses and meet the needs of human customers, your ultimate Boss is Jesus Christ.

All of this should have a profound effect on your motives on the job. Imagine as you tie your tie or put on your makeup in the morning asking yourself: How does my work relate to God? Am I going to work as His coworker? Do I see my work as part of His work in the world? And how does my work relate to others and the needs they have? Am I serving them? And am I faithfully providing for my family? Answering questions like these every day could infuse your work with a new enthusiasm and vitality!

How does your work relate to God? So often I meet people who tell me their employment is "just a job." They might as well say that their life is "just a life."

I realize that not every job is thrilling or spectacular. Nor must every job be particularly fulfilling. But what I hear these people saying is that their work is boring and insignificant.

This is tragic because God doesn't view your work as insignificant. As we have seen, He regards your job, and you, with great dignity and value. So should you!

Obviously, employers could do far more to remove some of the boredom of many tasks and to convey meaning and worth to their employees. But as a Christian you need to sign in at work as God's coworker and as an employee of Christ.

A business model. One way to gain this perspective is to ask: As God's coworker, how does my work serve other people and their needs?

Let me suggest a model to illustrate this perspective on work. Imagine a triangle with "customer" at the apex, "employees" at one point of the base, and "employer" at the other point.

These are the three human roles involved in most work world situations in our culture. And God desires that the needs of *each* should be met. The customer obviously has needs that you and your business are there to serve.

But if you are an employer, you also have a responsibility to serve the needs of your employees. They need adequate, appropriate compensation. But they also need proper, fair management; equitable employment policies; a reasonably safe work environment; appropriate tools, supplies, and equipment; regard for their lives outside of work, especially their families; and much more.

If you are an employee, you have a responsibility to serve the needs of your fellow employees and your employer. Your coworkers need you to do your part with excellence, with a spirit of cooperation, with honesty, and so forth. Likewise, your employer needs a dependable worker who is conscientious, puts forth his best effort, is honest, and gives value in exchange for his wages.

Using the model. Let's use this model in a real-life illustration. Suppose, for instance, that you are a single parent who works for the Department of Defense processing CHAMPUS claims. (CHAMPUS is a sort of medical insurance program for dependents of military personnel.) As God's coworker in the CHAMPUS system, how does your work serve the needs of others? I might suggest a few ways; you can think of others.

First, you directly help those who have filed claims. Any insurance program, military or otherwise, creates a monolithic system. The size is an asset in minimizing risk to the company and those it insures. But it sometimes works to the disadvantage of the individual who needs help from the system.

Now obviously, you cannot be responsible for every aspect of every claim that comes your way. Yet to the extent of your ability and responsibility, you can treat the claims that cross your desk as though they were crossing the desk of Christ.

Why? Because some sixteen-year-old mother of a sick infant whose husband is off on a ship somewhere sits at the other end of that claim. The form is her only way of communicating with the system. When it reaches you, is she dealing with an impersonal "system" or with a conscientious worker representing Christ? It all depends on your attitude at work.

So the mother, her child, and her husband need you to do your best work on their behalf. The same is true for every claim that comes your way.

But your coworkers also need you. This may sound laughable in such a huge enterprise, especially if your boss or others act as though "No one is indispensable here! There are plenty of other hires where you came from!"

Yet despite the inherent foolishness of this view, your work contributes to the overall objective of supplying health benefits to people. In your own way, you actually help keep the system running. And since the system provides income for you and your coworkers, you serve the needs of your coworkers.

You also serve the interests of American citizens and their government. Your work is part of what it takes to field a reliable defense. It would be difficult if not impossible to recruit qualified people for the service without providing medical benefits for their families. These dependents need such care, and in some small way you make that care possible.

Thus, your work ultimately has benefit for me and my family, and for anyone who lives and works under the protection of the United States.

Finally, your work obviously provides an income for you and your family. Since, in our illustration, you are a single parent, your child or children probably need daycare. Certainly you need housing, food, clothing, and transportation. Your work helps to provide for these needs.

Can you see how a biblical view of work redefines how you think about your job? As God's coworker, you can enter the workplace with a tremendous sense of God's presence and the conviction that God's power is at work in you to accomplish His work on behalf of other people.

Feel His pleasure! Perhaps you saw the movie, *Chariots of Fire*. You'll recall that the film tells the story of Eric Liddell, an Olympic runner from Scotland in the 1930s.

In the film, his sister questions why he intends to run in the Olympics rather than enter the ministry as a missionary. In a very dramatic moment, he turns to her and says, "Jenny, when I run, I feel God's pleasure."

His Way: "Your Worksyle"

That's an impressive appreciation of the presence of God. Liddell recognizes the fact that God wants to use him in the arena of running. God wants to do the same with you in your sphere of influence. When you do your work, He wants you to feel His pleasure.

Your work is an extension of God's work. That is why it has great dignity. But if it is God's work, then it must be done God's way. With dignity comes responsibility.

This means you need to work with a godly "workstyle." By "workstyle" I mean the way you do your work—the attitudes you express, the methods you employ, the strategies you use to achieve your results, and so forth. If the term "lifestyle" refers to how you typically live your life, "workstyle" has to do with how you typically do your work.

What should such a workstyle look like? So far in our study, I've tried to show that you as a layperson have the same dignity in your work as the pastor or missionary. But this implies that you also have the same responsibility to honor God in your work.

Character. Think about what this means for a moment. I am the president of Career Impact Ministries, a nonprofit Christian organization. What kind of behavior would you expect from me because I lead such an organization? How would you expect *me* to relate to my associates? Would you expect me to be selfish, ambitious, and excessively competitive? What would you expect in terms of the quality of the materials we produce? What would you expect of my language and the way I respond to people? How would you expect me to resolve conflicts? No doubt, you have a whole world of expectations for my conduct because of the position I hold.

And yet, I would challenge you that the same standards apply to you. Maybe not according to our culture, but certainly according to the Scriptures. You should pursue healthy relationships with the people you work with, just as I should. You should resolve conflicts with coworkers as peacefully and wisely as possible, just as I should. You should maintain high integrity, just as I should.

After all, you are doing God's work, just as I am. It is not just I who am doing God's work. You, too, are doing His work. And this gives you great dignity. But it also gives you great responsibility to do God's work, God's way.

This responsibility extends to a host of day-to-day work situations. Bill and I have identified at least ninety "critical issues" as we call them, areas in which Christians need to live with ethical distinction. These include matters of integrity, relationships on the job, hiring and firing, the quality of one's work, and many more. In areas like these, you need to distinguish yourself by your character.

Two workstyles. By way of illustration, Bill recalls taking his car to a mechanic for service. He had asked around, and someone had suggested this particular mechanic. "He'll do a good job. He's a Christian," this reference had said.

Bill asked the mechanic to check his brakes, check his carburetor, and change the oil, but not the filter. Yet upon returning, Bill discovered that the shop had given him a complete tune-up, new brakes, and a new oil filter! The total came to more than $400!

Needless to say, Bill disputed both the work and the price. But what struck him most was the slipshod performance and questionable ethics of the shop, run as it was by a believer.

By contrast, Bill took his car on another occasion to a different mechanic, also a Christian. In this case, the fellow wrote down in detail what was to be performed, what the estimated charges would be, and where to contact Bill if additional costs seemed likely.

The work was completed on time and according to the agreed upon charges. In fact, part of the job had included replenishing the freon in the air-conditioning. But once the mechanic had hooked up the gauges and so forth, he had found the level to be fine. He didn't charge for that. "Can't charge for what don't need fixin'," he explained.

This man impressed Bill by his workstyle, and by the quality and honesty of his work. He was doing God's work, God's way. In fact, I submit that in the transaction between Bill and that mechanic, the central question from God's perspective was: Did the mechanic service the car as though Christ Himself were wielding the tools? Remember that God will someday evaluate the performance and motives of that mechanic (Ephesians 6:7–8).

Authority. Another crucial aspect of workstyle is our attitude toward authority. We've already seen that as a Christ-follower, you work for Jesus; He is your

Boss. But He demands that you respect and obey whoever is in authority over you on earth (Ephesians 6:54):

> Slaves, be obedient to those who are your masters according to the flesh, with fear and trembling, in the sincerity of your heart, as to Christ; not by way of eyeservice, as men-pleasers, but as slaves of Christ, doing the will of God from the heart.

Or as Peter told his readers (1 Peter 2:18):

> Servants, be submissive to your masters with all respect, not only to those who are good and gentle, but also to those who are unreasonable.

In practical terms, this means abiding by the rules and policies of your company, and carrying out the orders of those above you. It also includes obeying the law. I'm well aware that there are special cases where we might question whether blind obedience is the best policy. And of course rules, policies, and laws sometimes need to be revised or done away with.

But these few exceptions ought never to justify our ignoring authority, even authority we do not respect. No matter how despicable those over us may behave, we must see that standing behind them is Christ Himself. Naturally He takes no pleasure in despotic or dishonest leaders.

But neither does He think much of disobedient or devious employees.

The point is that the way we do our work says everything about how seriously we take our faith. In fact, Paul claims that when we work with a godly workstyle and live with an ethically distinctive lifestyle, we "adorn the doctrine of God." That is, our character and our work paint a beautiful picture of Christlikeness. (See Titus 2:9–10.) This is doing God's work, God's way.

His Results: Our Outlook

But when we do God's work, God's way, we can also trust Him for the results. This is a remarkably liberating concept, both for those who tend toward boredom at work and for those who find work to be extremely stimulating.

Boredom. First of all, the idea that God is using you to accomplish a specific purpose can be a real help if you question the significance of your career.

Three years ago, a dentist studied the same ideas that I have presented in this book. Time and time again ever since, he has told me that these biblical principles of work have revolutionized his feelings about his job.

You may know that dentists have one of the highest suicide rates of any profession. It's a career that has the kind of routine and monotony that make it a high-stress occupation. And this particular individual had been experiencing quite a bit of that.

But as he began to think about his work as being God's work, and as he attempted to do it God's way, he developed a sense of destiny and calling. He perceived that God had called him to contribute to the physical well-being of people, and that his skills as a dentist contributed to the health of the people who came to see him.

In short, he saw his work, dentistry, as a ministry. This has helped him in the midst of his routine, everyday work.

And so it is for all of us. We all find aspects of our job to be very mundane, or perhaps even distasteful. And yet, when we realize that we are in the job because God has placed us there, it lends a sense of dignity, as well as destiny, to our work.

Careerism. But this saw cuts in the other direction, too. Perhaps you are like many in our culture, in that you find work to be fulfilling and exhilarating. This is wonderful—to a point.

Unfortunately, many people place more expectations on their careers than any career can possibly fulfill. If you are one of these, you probably have a very unrealistic view of the product of your labor.

Ecclesiastes points to the futility that marks so much of our labor. The book explains that we work amid endless cycles of life, so that whatever we do has pretty much been done before, and will need to be done again after we're gone.

Hence, we should never look to the product of our work to give us ultimate meaning and dignity.

That is not to say that the product of our work has no meaning or dignity—only that it need not form the basis of our personal worth and significance.

But unfortunately, this is precisely what work has come to mean for too many of us. The outcome depends on us, and we depend on the outcome. This turns work into an idol, and idols make harsh masters.

By contrast, those who put Christ first in their careers find a refreshing sense of release from the slavery of work. You may have discovered that while hard work satisfies, overwork destroys. Yet overwork is the inevitable slavery that captures the person who believes, "It all depends on me!"

Winning isn't the only thing. A few years ago, a major NFL coach retired. Following the news conference at which he announced his resignation, a reporter pulled him aside. "Coach," he was asked, "how is it that you are retiring from professional football after only three or four years, while men like [the late] Tom Landry, the coach of the Dallas Cowboys, [was] in the game for twenty or more years?"

The retiree paused for a moment, and then looked the reporter in the eye and said, "Well, as you know, Tom Landry [was] a Christian. He love[d] to win about as much as anyone I have ever met. But Tom realize[d] that the biggest thing in life is not football."

That's a profound comment! And Landry [had] a profound testimony, in that his faith [lent] perspective to his work. Over and over the press carry reports about the personal side of Coach Landry. To a man they praise him for pursuing a high level of excellence, for having a high regard for good coaching, and for turning in as professional a performance as he [could]. And yet they also report that for Landry, there [were] bigger things to life than just winning.

A man like Landry [was] able to rest and relax because he [knew] that his job [was] to do God's work, God's way, and to trust God with the results. Not that he [was] excited when he loses; he hate[d] losing. We all do. And yet he realize[d] that losing a football game is not the ultimate disaster. He avoid[ed] that stress because he ha[d] a biblical view of the outcome of his work.

Who is in control? God, in His sovereignty, may select you to go through adversity in your career. He would allow that to show a watching world the reality of your faith and how you deal with adversity as His coworker. On the other side, He might shower you with incredible success and achievement, again to show a watching world how you handle it.

Either way, the outcome of your work is largely out of your control. Not totally. You have some measure of control over what happens. You must make decisions, perform as best as you can, monitor your character and ethics.

But so much is beyond your direct control: the overall economy; decisions made by foreign governments; the value of the dollar; the choices of your coworkers. You have no way of controlling these events.

Consequently, you must ultimately trust God for the results of your labor, and do whatever is within your limited sphere of power to promote a God-honoring outcome. But having this perspective can be a tremendous relief from the stress and anxiety that plague our culture.

CONCLUSION

His work. His way. His results. Adopting such a perspective could transform the way you approach your job each day. It could eliminate the chasm between your work and your spiritual life, bringing them back together into a meaningful whole. It could mean working with a sense that you are participating in the highest and noblest thing any man or woman could ever do—God's work.

from the editors of *The Life@Work Journal*

. . .

Michael Novak got the expected response when people learned he was writing a book about the role of religion in the lives of business leaders: Isn't capitalism the religion for the business world? And isn't capitalism all about making money and getting ahead no matter the moral consequences? And what do business leaders know, or care, about God?

In a culture in which image is everything, the image of business was anything but spiritual when *Business as a Calling* was published in 1996. Novak, a theologian and former U.S. ambassador, has written more than twenty-five books on theology, politics, economics, and culture, and he was acutely aware of the gulf between this perception and reality.

Novak doesn't have some Pollyanna view of the business world. "Immoral acts do occur in business," he writes. "But to behave immorally is neither necessary to nor conducive to business success."

Novak's book serves to destroy the myth of the greedy businessman and emphasizes the moral force and sacred nature of business. He establishes the reality that most religious people work in business. In other words, business is their calling.

But what is calling? Beyond expressing the connection between the spiritual and business worlds, Novak successfully grapples with this question, coming up with solid answers. Using a series of biographies (Paul F. Oreffice, retired chairman of Dow Chemical Company; investing legend Sir John Templeton; Kenneth Lay, CEO, Enron Corp, etc.), Novak illustrates four primary principals of calling. Calling is personal, unique, and specific; specific callings require specific talents; true callings are enjoyed; and callings are not easy to discover.

We glean from Novak's opening chapter that a personal and specific understanding of calling in our lives is absolutely essential, but is often difficult to know.

Besides identifying four principals of a calling, Novak gives his take on such questions as "Can a calling remain tacit?" and "Can a calling be entirely secular?" He lays the groundwork for an understanding of why having a calling makes such a tremendous difference in our everyday life at work.

3 What Is a Calling?

from *Business as a Calling* by Michael Novak

Vocation (Lat. *vocatio*, a calling): the function or career toward which one believes himself to be called.

—New World Dictionary 2d college ed.

The earning of money within the modern economic order is, so long as it is done legally, the result and the expression of virtue and proficiency in a calling. . . . And in truth this peculiar idea, so familiar to us today, but in reality so little a matter of course, of one's duty in a calling, is what is most characteristic of the social ethic of capitalist culture, and is in a sense the fundamental basis of it. . . . Now it is unmistakable that even in the German word *Beruf* and perhaps still more clearly in the English calling, a religious conception, that of a task set by God, is at least suggested.

—Max Weber

THERE IS SOMETHING about business no one may have told you in business school or economics class. Something important.

Maybe more important than anything else in your life, except your marriage and your children.

It is the answer to this question: During their busy lives, what gives people in business their greatest pleasure, and what at the end of their lives gives them their greatest satisfaction?

Whatever it is, don't we often call this "fulfillment"? But fulfillment of what? Not exactly a standing order that we placed ourselves. We didn't give ourselves the personalities, talents, or longings we were born with. When we fulfill these—these gifts from beyond ourselves—it is like fulfilling something we were meant to do. It is a sense of having uncovered our personal destiny, a sense of having been able to contribute something worthwhile to the common public life, something that would not have been there without us—and, more than that, something that we were good at and something we enjoyed.

Even if we do not always think of it that way, each of us was given a calling—by fate, by chance, by destiny, by God. Those who are lucky have found it.

CALLINGS

But what exactly is a calling—or (for those who insist) an identity? How would we know one if we saw it? What do you look for, if you wish to find your own?

One good way is to mull over examples from the lives of others. First, though, we need to understand that in our culture (vast and many-faceted as it is), we expect each calling (each personal identity) to be unique. No two people have exactly the same calling. That is why we need to mull over many examples if we are trying to apply them to ourselves. None will ever quite fit; some may suggest useful clues, and some may leave us cold.

Here are several stories of callings I've encountered over the years, including one about myself. Limited pretty much to the field of business, they should give a larger sense of what it means to heed a calling.

• M. Scott Peck, M.D., the famous author, tells the story of a young enlisted man in Okinawa who served under him as a practicing therapist. Peter was unusually good at his assignment, and Dr. Peck tried to get him to enter graduate school on his return to the United States. "You're a fine therapist. I could help you get into a good master's program. Your GI Bill would pay for it."

The young soldier said he wanted to start a business. Dr. Peck admits to being "aghast."

As Dr. Peck began reciting the advantages of a career in psychotherapy, he was stopped cold by the young enlisted man: "Look, Scotty, can't you get it in your head that not everyone is like you?" Not every one wants to be a psychotherapist.

Callings are like that. To identify them, two things are normally required: the God-given ability to do the job, and (equally God-given) enjoyment in doing it because of your desire to do it.

• In my case, I studied for the Catholic priesthood for twelve and a half years, at the end of which (after a long, dark struggle) I came to know clearly that the priesthood was not my calling. I abandoned my studies five months before ordination. I enjoyed every minute of those twelve-plus years and am everlastingly grateful for them. I loved my friends and colleagues and had many great priests around as models (plus one or two likeable odd ones, who for my generation of students provided a treasure house of anecdotes). I had the advantages of superb spiritual direction and, toward the end, an outside psychotherapist to help me sort things out. Himself a silent Sphinx, he made me sort it out myself. In the end, though, the answer came most clearly during months of silent prayer.

Callings are sometimes like that.

I not only felt much inner resistance to the priesthood—insisting that this was not my vocation—but also an inner drive of my being toward becoming a writer, being involved in politics and social change, trying my hand at fiction, exploring new territories in philosophy and theology. All of these ventures would involve me, I knew, in controversy. It would be enough to defend myself, it seemed, without implicating the whole church (as were I a priest, I would). I needed to be a bit more of a Lone Ranger than a priest ought to be.

• John Templeton, founder of the Templeton Growth Fund and perhaps the greatest investor of our time, whom in recent years I have come to know and admire tremendously, told *Forbes* magazine recently that when he was young, he had wanted to become a missionary. From his early days in Winchester, Tennessee, and continuing through his years at Yale and then at Oxford as a Rhodes scholar, he had been a devout young man. At Yale and Oxford, he met a number of Christian missionaries home from abroad and recognized, finally, that he didn't have that kind of stuff.

"I realized that they had more talent as missionaries than I did," he remembers. "But I also realized that I was more talented with money than they were. So I decided to devote myself to helping the missionaries financially." In fact, Sir John (he was knighted by Queen Elizabeth in 1987 for his wide-ranging accomplishments) pioneered in the field of international investing, typically being the first to invest where things looked bleakest and showing extraordinary patience.

His financial success has been amazing. So also has been his worldwide philanthropy. In retirement, he is carrying his philanthropy to new areas—chiefly those concerned with ideas and the formation of the virtue and character necessary for human freedom

Incidentally, to this day, he flies tourist class, preferring to invest the savings he retains.

One can see in Sir John's several books that he has drawn great drafts of objectivity, perspective, patience, and calm judgment from time devoted every day to prayer. He treats his lifetime occupation, global investing, as a calling God made him to do his best at.

• Edward Crosby Johnson II, another talented investor, is best known for starting Fidelity Investments, today the largest mutual fund company in the country. Known in investment circles as "Mister Johnson," he was the grandson of both a doctor and a missionary. Mister Johnson's father, Samuel Johnson, followed neither the medical nor the ministerial route. Instead, he was drafted into a family retailing business, which he never enjoyed. What really interested Samuel were his hobbies, including the study of pre-Christian religions.

Mister Johnson inherited his father's

interest in religion, especially Eastern religious philosophies, because they gave him another way of looking at the world and understanding people. But it was his father's lack of enthusiasm for his work—compared to the passion he had for his hobbies that convinced Mister Johnson early on that he wanted to do something he was good at and enjoyed. Initially, he chose law as a profession, but he soon discovered law wasn't his calling. Investing (and the psychology of the stock market) was. To him, the stock market was "like a beautiful woman, endlessly fascinating, endlessly complex, always changing, always mystifying."

In 1943, he decided to turn his hobby into a full-time career by buying the management contract for (or the right to manage) a small Boston-based mutual fund, Fidelity Fund. Thus, Fidelity Investments began by one man's pursuing his natural interests. In the 1940s, mutual funds—separate legal entities that pooled the money of many small investors—were still catching on. What they offered individuals was diversification and professional management at a reasonable cost—something previously available only to the wealthy.

Providing a service that had never before been readily available delighted Mister Johnson. He wrote to his Harvard classmates in 1945: "It is a real thrill to try to give the small investor—of which our companies are mainly comprised—as good a job of investing as the big man gets." That thought nourished him throughout his life as he increased the range of funds available to small investors.

• Kenneth Lay, chairman and chief executive officer of the largest natural gas company in the United States (and one of the largest in the world), Enron Corp of Houston, some time ago announced publicly his company's vision: "To become the first natural gas major . . . the most innovating and reliable provider of clean energy worldwide." His greatest inward satisfaction, however, has a somewhat different focus.

"In my own case," Lay confided, "I grew up the son of a Baptist minister. From this background, I was fully exposed to not only legal behavior but moral and ethical behavior and what that means from the standpoint of leading organizations and people. I was, and am, a strong believer that one of the most satisfying things in life is to create a highly moral and ethical environment in which every individual is allowed and encouraged to realize their God-given potential. There are few things more satisfying than to see individuals reach levels of performance that they would have thought was virtually impossible for themselves."

• Lorraine Miller spent two years as a VISTA volunteer in North Carolina, and a career in business was the furthest thing from her mind. At that time, she thought that "creating a profit also created poverty." After winning the Utah Small Business Person of the Year Award, she won the same award for the entire United States in 1994. She didn't get started in business because she wanted to make money; because her first boss had offended her, she wanted to be her own boss (incidentally, one of the three most frequently cited motives among small businessmen). Back in Utah she had noticed that neither outdoor nurseries nor florists supplied the market with potted house plants and decided to spend half her $2,000 in savings on a small stock of such plants in a store she named the Glass Menagerie. Every weekend she drove twelve hours each way to California in her VW van in search of unusual plants. "When you're 25 years old, you can work all day and drive all night, and still have plenty of energy," she told *Nation's Business*. For the first five years, her income was below the poverty line, and she knew nothing about filing regular government reports mandated by labor laws, since as a self-employed person she didn't have to know.

About five years after her start-up, she moved into a new store under a new name, Cactus & Tropicals, hired her first employee, built a greenhouse, and began selling wholesale to grocery chains. She learned quickly enough that margins are higher in retail and went back to that, while starting an ambitious new program on the side: taking care of plants (now 2 million of them) on maintenance contract for commercial establishments. She was then employing thirty-five persons. She still wasn't in it for the money.

When she was told, on receiving her national and statewide awards, that she had "peaked," she got energized. She began planning to increase her business from $1 million to $5 million in sales within three years. Now she was in it for the money: "I want to create a space where my employees can grow, too, and to do that for them—helping them with their educations and things like that—I have to make a lot of money."

You can pay yourself poverty wages at the beginning, but you can't find and keep good workers except by paying good wages and benefits. Making more money didn't make her life easier, of course. She went into business to be her own boss; now her business is her boss, and it's a demanding one at that. But this business is hers.

• Building a corporate community of a certain type was also the deepest satisfaction of the business career of Robert Malott, retired chairman of the FMC Corporation in Chicago. At his retirement, he was lauded for a number of highly significant achievements in the firm. "One can be thanked," he later noted, "for successful events, but to be recognized for establishing a 'corporate culture' about which one can be proud, is much more significant." This satisfaction was driven home to him by a manager of his whom he had lauded at a retirement party a little earlier than his own. The insight arrived via a handwritten note:

> Bob, thanks so much for your kind words at my retirement party. The praise and credit you granted me was quite thoughtful and much appreciated. It has been a privilege to be associated with you for the past 20 years. The high standards of performance you set, coupled with your spotless integrity, made me better than I might otherwise have been. Although you graciously gave me credit for many things, it was only your leadership, guidance and unrelenting demand to do the best possible job that allowed me to do what I did. It is a truism that the character of an organization reflects the character of the person at the top, and all credit goes to you for making FMC truly great over the years you were at the helm. It was a wonderful journey; thanks so much for all your help along the way.

Bob Malott cherishes that letter as much as the memory of any other business achievement. Some men are born leaders and get their greatest pleasure from the *esprit de corps* they can build up,

in the task-driven enterprise that a business is. That, too, is a kind of calling.

• A quite different angle is taken by David Packard of Hewlett-Packard, who got his start in a garage in Palo Alto. Packard's public language is typically quite secular, as when he discussed why a company exists in the first place: "Why are we here? I think many people assume, wrongly, that a company exists solely to make money." Packard knows that making money is an important result of a company's existence, if the company is any good. But a result isn't a cause. "We have to go deeper and find the real reasons for our being. As we investigate this, we inevitably come to the conclusion that a group of people get together and exist as an institution that we call a company so that they are able to accomplish something collectively that they could not accomplish separately—they make a contribution to society, a phrase which sounds trite but is fundamental."

Part of the business vocation, then, is getting together and forming a task-oriented community—a community, in other words, not to satisfy all needs but to get a few specific things done—done for the public, "to make a contribution to society" that no one person could make alone but must be made by many together. Most business callings are not for loners, although for them there are some niche businesses and many niches within most business firms. On the whole, a certain instinct for community and working well with others is highly desirable, if not required. Good social habits—and even social graces—are significant assets.

But Packard's point is deeper than this. "You can look around and still see underlying drives" at work in businesses. These come "largely from a desire to do something else—to make a product—to give a service—generally, to do something which is of value." "The real reason for Hewlett-Packard's existence is to provide something that is unique." What drives inventors of a new product or service is the desire to bring this new thing before the public. They want to prove to themselves and to others that it is as valuable as at one point they may have been alone in thinking that it would be.

Never underestimate the creative pleasure that drives many who find their calling in business. Walking an interested stranger through their operations, they take as much pride in what they have built as any *diva* in a standing-ovation performance at La Scala. They remember what it was like when all this was nothing but a dream (concerning which, many sober people told them they would lose their shirt). Like the Creator in Genesis, they look over what they have made and find it good—but usually with a restless eye, trying to make it better.

• My friend Joe Jacobs, founder of Jacobs Engineering in Los Angeles (and author of the instructive book, *The Compassionate Conservative)*, is bubbly and joyous about the fun he had building up his business. He has a sign on his desk, "BABE RUTH STRUCK OUT 1330 TIMES." Asked, he is glad to tell you about the many times that Joe Jacobs struck out too. At one point, when he tried to retire too early, things started to go wrong—some bad decisions were made—under the new chief executive officer, and personnel relations also deteriorated badly. Joe had really intended to retire and so stayed away from the company. By the time he was persuaded to return, after about four years, bankruptcy was near at hand. He had two choices: accept bankruptcy or cut personnel severely and swim as strongly as he could for solid land far ahead. Those he had to cut were guys he had hired and enjoyed being with, having known their wives and kids and all their family circumstances for years. The cutting was, he says, "gut-wrenching," the hardest thing he had ever had to do. Sink or swim, he kept telling himself. His only comfort—it wasn't much at the time—was that if he succeeded, he would save a good many other jobs; if he did nothing, the firm, and everybody with it, would go down.

In retrospect, Joe came to think he hadn't made all the right choices either. There were some people he let go who probably would have done a better job than one or two of those he kept. But the firm came out of it all right: much smaller and with bare cupboards for a while, but later stronger than ever. It's the pain, Joe suggests, that makes the later happiness of having built the firm so poignantly satisfying. You can't forget, later, all the costs, close brushes with disaster, bad days and nights. The hard and stormy things are as much a part of a calling as the cloudless ones. Emerging on the other side, you understand accomplishment in ways that in youth you did not expect. The 1330 strikeouts make the homers sweeter.

One reason people like a business calling, then, is the challenges it offers. They like the feeling, toward the end of life, that they were severely tested and accomplished something—something that they can see, that they know has made a contribution. They know this, because people use what they have provided, sometimes praise it, value it, pay good money for it—and are glad to do so. Joe can see the buildings, refineries, and countless other projects his firm has put up. He takes pride in their quality. But I think that most of all, he has enjoyed going through the hardships with his team and his association with them. Joe is both a people person and an excellence person—an engineer with lots of compassion. (He defines compassion by whether it helps the beneficiary to better his or her condition, or only makes the giver feel good; he

is pretty passionate about the harm the latter does.)

• The unsung heroes of business, of course, are those in middle management who, when things get tough, as at Jacobs Engineering some years ago and in the current wave of restructuring, are the ones let go. Talk about the firm going down; what about their families? James H. Billington, Jr., an alert and inquisitive Episcopal seminarian who worked for five years in a large corporation—his aim was to form a ministry for people in business—has written eloquently:

The middle manager faces a double bind. First, he is subject to the same religious/cultural conditioning as everyone else in a business, subtly teaching him that he is just in it for the money, that making money is bad, etc. But he is also subject to the disrespect of the business elite, who have been taught in the business schools that middle management is the reason that American companies cannot compete. But in fact most Americans who work in business are still middle managers. And middle management still makes up most of the jobs in business.

Most people in business are neither tightening bolts on engines nor sitting in the president's office. "Most people," Billington reminds us, "are still writing invoices or computer codes, running a department or sales force—working to implement plans that they did not create." They are still most of the people in the business world. "And NOWHERE," Billington concludes, "in the business literature that I have found is there any recognition of the legitimate, substantive and honorable contributions of the middle manager."

Well, I have found many and eloquent tributes to such people and their indispensability—on their retirement. Heads of firms certainly know who keeps their company surging ahead, or at least on even keel, and how helpless they are if their middle managers are incompetent or inattentive. Most pride themselves on recruiting, motivating, and amply rewarding top-flight managers, including a bunch of them capable of replacing the top honcho. Managerial talent is rare, and the extra margin of inventiveness and courage that make a great leader is even rarer.

Moreover, being a middle manager is not primarily a way station on the way to the top. Probably everyone wants at first to test themselves against that possibility; but, realistically, most middle managers expect some advancement over a lifetime, higher salaries and bonuses, and most of all the ever higher respect of their peers, while expecting to remain middle managers (vice-president tops) until retirement. Middle management, many know early, is their calling. They want to be super good at it. They want to make a

contribution. Most of all, they need to know in their own minds that they have done so.

Second, their daily bread is recognition from their peers and those who work with them that they are very good at what they do. But they also want, as humans properly do, recognition from higher ups.

As the world goes, except for the few at the top (deservedly or undeservedly), most people do not get the recognition they have earned. "That's what's wrong with the world," an otherworldly and happy nun, Sister Gervase, told me in seventh grade. "People don't compliment other people enough. They would change the world if they did."

More than anyone else in business, middle managers are in the position to compliment those who work under them every day. The spirit they give the firm— if they are sustained by their superiors— *is* the firm in action. They are the chief community builders. They give (or fail to give) the firm its human character.

They are also the main trustees of the integrity and moral practices of the firm. They are its moral and intellectual spine. Business is a noble field of work, and they are its chief day-to-day guardians. By their leadership, they make their bosses look good—or bad—and, in a slightly different way, they also make those who work under them look good—or bad. For all the solid, concrete things that business does for communities and for the entire nation, they are the down-to-earth leaders most responsible. For their success, they depend a lot on good leadership from the top, but it may also be argued that good leadership at the top depends even more disproportionately on them.

• The advertising executive Emilie Griffin presents another aspect of the business calling in her good book, *The Reflexive Executive*. It is clear, she writes, "that the best entrepreneurial visions are founded in love." She uses the example of Phyllis Jordan, founder of PJ's Coffee and Tea Company, a regional enterprise that franchises coffee shops. PJ's is built around two different insights, each of them expressing in plain English an aspect of what religious people would call love—not the sentiment, but the effort to build community.

Phyllis Jordan explains why she started PJ's in this fashion:

- What I was really attracted to was being in the retail business. . . .
- I had a friend who was in the coffee business, that gave me the information I needed, the know-how. . . .
- But I think that sense of her in [her coffee shop], offering a product which was a shared experience with a friend, that was what attracted me to coffee. I wanted to see people talking to the people they've come with, or maybe the people they haven't come with. I don't think we can document this,

but I know there are major social changes going on, including a return to basics, maybe concern about the environment, a number of things that are converging to make neighborhood experiences and simple values very important. I think specialty coffee in the U.S. is part of that.

This camaraderie in the coffee shop—a neighborhood place for a little sharing—is the central insight that animates Phyllis Jordan and PJ's, as other central insights animate scores of thousands of other entrepreneurs.

But Jordan has another central theme in mind, too—a worldwide one. She served for a year as president of the Specialty Coffee Association of America and saw another level of community at work:

The [specialty coffee] association brings together people from growing countries and exporters and farmers with roasters and retailers in a trade association in which the focus is the product, and not on which part of the business you're in, and in that way it's a very cooperative effort, one that produces win-win solutions for growers and manufacturers and everybody. We think the organization can only work if everybody along the chain wins.

Here Emilie Griffin herself comments that "words such as these from a regional entrepreneur may have about them a sense of the commonplace, the ordinary." To her eye, though, this creative urge of enterprise can become a saintly one—in the perfectly natural sense of saintliness: "When the reflective executive strives to live out his or her inner vision through a sharing of values, not only with co-workers and customers, not only with colleagues and others in industry, but with the world in the largest possible definition or conception of which he or she is capable."

Jordan may not want her words to fly so high, and yet what she does matters more than what she says. She enjoys building community, on more than one level. That sort of calling seems to please something deep within her. She sees her daily work—"what I liked was the tremendous variety of tasks"—in a far larger framework. Entrepreneurs often see a little more in humble things than other people do. Their characteristic habit is sharp discernment.

• In this vein, Paul F. Oreffice, retired chairman of the Dow Chemical Company, says that his greatest satisfaction in business was working with and knowing the "guys" in middle management—always on his lookout for talent. He remembers spotting a thirty-one-year-old researcher who became a "gigantic" strength for the company. His greatest pride lies in having spotted eight special talents among younger fellows in the company in 1975

and pushing them along. From this list of eight, he said with satisfaction almost twenty years later, seven were now in the top leadership of the firm.

"Never chew out a colleague in public," he says. "The idea is to create a team. And to form in them the habit of not bringing you their problems. The only question I had for each of them was, 'What's your *solution?*' They have to be the ones to make the decisions. They have to learn to talk things through in a team—one brain is never as good as four or five brains."

He also says: "If a guy doesn't look at business as a vocation, he's not gonna make it. And the vocation changes as you grow. For me, it was one thing at 30, another at 50 and at 60. The one consistent thing—I loved challenges."

Paul was born in Italy, and as a child emigrated with his parents to Ecuador. His first business success was turning a small chemical company in Brazil into the nation's second largest in the field. He was twenty-eight when he started on that challenge.

He loved his years at Dow, turning down offers to work elsewhere, always being given new challenges. He likes working for a company—"founded by a farm boy from Nebraska"—that had a tradition of never, under any circumstances, paying bribes or going under the table with officials. "The rule was there: That made it easy for those who came later. No ifs, ands, or buts."

It is obvious that Mr. Oreffice—twice an immigrant, to Latin America and to the United States—loved his time in business.

• John W. Rowe of New England Electric System remembers thinking that money is not what really motivated him when, one day, between two jobs, he was standing at a newsstand in an airport. He saw a copy of *Playboy* and distinctly recalls telling himself that he could understand people buying it and enjoying it, "but I don't really wish to make my living selling it." It's important to value the business you're in and to take satisfaction from providing its services or goods to others. At the end of the day, you want to respect what you do. In a certain sense, our work *is* us. We get into it, and it gets into us.

There is nothing wrong with wanting to make a good living, or even in seeking out a life of business that produces good rewards. But not all ways of gaining money are equal. Better than inheriting money is to earn it through inventiveness and hard work—or at least to make something better of it, using it well. Business is about creating goods and services, jobs and benefits, and new wealth that didn't exist before. In choosing a line of work, you want to find the one that suits the kind of person you are—the individual you are. Mr. Rowe is very much oriented toward free market ideas, although his business (natural gas) is a halfway house between entrepreneurship and nonprofit

government activity. In this mix, the government and politics side can be especially irritating, because it seems to be moved more often by transient emotion than by long-term reason. Perhaps this explains the slight vehemence Mr. Rowe showed when a pastor in Maine came by to see him when he was at an earlier job with a utility company.

After discussing the main item on his agenda, the pastor asked Mr. Rowe, more or less by way of chitchat, how he liked his job. Mr. Rowe replied: "Oh, I like it. It gives me a chance to work with people I respect, who know a lot that I don't know. I get to protect capital from some of the depredations of government. Most of all, I like to think I'm helping to keep an important part of our economic infrastructure in place, in support of other people's opportunities."

Mr. Rowe still remembers the stunned look on the minister's face: "You mean you have a calling?"

FOUR CHARACTERISITCS OF A CALLING

What have we learned about callings from these examples? At least four points should now be clear, about callings in general and those in business in particular.

First, each calling is unique to each individual. Not everyone wants to be a psychiatrist, as Dr. Peck discovered. Nor, for that matter, does everyone want to work in business. Each of us is as unique in our calling as we are in being made in the image of God. (It would take an infinite number of human beings, St. Thomas Aquinas once wrote, to mirror back the infinite facets of the Godhead. Each person reflects only a small—but beautiful—part of the whole.)

Second, a calling requires certain preconditions. It requires more than desires; it requires talent. Not everyone can be, simply by desiring it, an opera singer, or professional athlete, or leader of a large enterprise. For a calling to be right, it must fit our abilities. Another precondition is love—not just love of the final product but, as the essayist Logan Pearsall Smith once put it, "The test of a vocation is love of drudgery it involves." Long hours, frustrations, small steps forward, struggles: unless these too are welcomed with a certain joy, the claim to being called has a hollow ring.

Third, a true calling reveals its presence by the enjoyment and sense of renewed energies its practice yields us. This does not mean that sometimes we do not groan inwardly at the weight of the burdens imposed on us or that we never feel reluctance about reentering bloody combat. Facing hard tasks necessarily exacts dread. Indeed, there are times when we wish we did not have to face every burden our calling imposes on us. Still, finding ourselves where we are and with the responsibilities we bear, we know it is our duty—part of what we were meant to do—to soldier on.

Enjoying what we do is not always a feeling of enjoyment; it is sometimes the gritty resolution a man or woman shows in doing what must be done—perhaps with inner dread and yet without whimpering self-pity. These are things a grown man or woman must do. There is an odd satisfaction in bearing certain pains. The young men who died defending the pass at Thermopylae, Aristotle intimates, died happy. But he was not describing their feelings, only their knowledge that they did what brave young Spartans ought to do to protect their city, no matter the taste of ashes in their mouths.

A fourth truth about callings is also apparent: they are not usually easy to discover. Frequently, many false paths are taken before the satisfying path is at last uncovered. Experiments, painful setbacks, false hopes, discernment, prayer, and much patience are often required before the light goes on.

Businesspeople who have found their callings will recognize all of these things, if only tacitly. Against sometimes dreary opposition, they know their callings to be morally legitimate, even noble. Listen again to the testimony heard in this chapter. The point of business is "to accomplish something collectively," "to make a contribution to society," "to do something which is of value," "to provide something that is unique," "to test a person's talents and character," "to build community." This is unambiguously moral language that reflects moral reality.

At least four themes concerning the moral nature of business have thus far risen to the surface: (1) Business is able to build praiseworthy forms of community. (2) A life in business is creative; it can transform the conditions of human life dramatically and for the better (or the worse). (3) Business is a source of endless personal challenge, testing intellectual and moral mettle in the crucible of practicality. (4) Those practicing it often see business as a way of giving back to society, both through the goods and services it produces and in philanthropy, through the new wealth it generates.

We need to answer two more questions about the nature of a calling. Can a calling remain implicit and unspoken? Is there such a thing as a secular, nonreligious calling?

CAN A CALLING REMAIN TACIT?

I know from talking to and corresponding with businesspeople that many have never been asked whether they regard what they do as a calling. They don't think about themselves that way. That has not been the language of the business schools, the economics textbooks, or the secularized public speech of our time. (In previous generations, public speech in America was frequently biblical and Shakespearean.) But most of them, they say, do start mulling the idea of calling once it is raised. Some confess that they

could think of what they do as a calling, even if they have not. That would not be much of a reach from what they have already been doing. It's just one of those things that, so far, too few people say.

But they could, and it would be better if they did. It would give them a greater sense of being part of a noble profession. It would raise their own esteem for what they do—and no doubt stimulate their imaginations about how they might gain greater and deeper satisfactions from doing it. It would help tie them more profoundly to traditions going far back into the past, in seeing their own high place in the scheme of things. The human project is a universal project. We are involved in bringing the Creator's work to its intended fulfillment by being co-creators in a very grand project, indeed. In this, we are tied to the whole human race.

In particular, business has a special role to play in bringing hope—and not only hope, but actual economic progress to the billion or so truly indigent people on this planet. Business is, bar none, the best real hope of the poor. And that is one of the noblest callings inherent in business activities: to raise up the poor.

CAN A CALLING BE ENTIRELY SECULAR?

Yes. That answer rests on the evidence of fact. Among America's well-educated elites especially, many people do think in nonreligious terms. (Frequently they do not recognize that many of today's secular terms are derived from religious precedents. However, we would not speak of secularization unless our basic terms had first been religious.) As far as they can see, there is no one or nothing calling them. Indeed, they know from experience the difference between going down one road in search of their own proper career for a while and recognizing it as a mistake, then turning in a new direction. They know what it is like to "find themselves"—to find the activities they are good at and thoroughly enjoy and feel at home doing. They are quite capable of using what seems to them to be a wholly secular language. In addition, religious language may make some of them uncomfortable; it feels false.

For most citizens of the world, however, the background language of their self-awareness springs from the originality and distinctive dramaturgy of the biblical vision of cosmic history. For some three thousand years, both unbelievers and those affected by the biblical vision (the Koran accepts the Jewish and Christian testaments as its starting place) have engaged in rival picturings and theory building in trying to interpret human life. But we all must deal with the same facts of human experience, so there is much overlap in our interpretations. It is fair to say that how the West thinks about life has been mainly shaped (for a majority of

the peoples of the world) by Judaism, Christianity, and Islam.

Even the philosophical riches of pagan Greece and Rome, buried under the ferocity of the barbarian invasions from the fourth century on, were recovered for the West under the aegis of Jewish, Christian, and Muslim rulers, scholars, and artists. In all three of these great shaping forces of the human imagination, moreover, one fundamental point is the same: the Creator of all things knows the name of each of us—knows thoroughly, better than we do ourselves, what is in us, for he put it there and intends for us to do something with it—something that meshes with his intentions for many other people. This proposition, suitably rephrased, is capable of standing as a distinctively secular world view.

Nothing is by chance, these religions teach, in the sense of being beyond his knowing of it, although certainly in life there are many crossing lines of contingency that set off those sparks of surprise, spontaneity, and unplannedness that we call chance. In this respect, religious believers and secular unbelievers might see the same realities but interpret their meaning differently.

Further, for the three major religions mentioned, God does not pull puppets' strings. He made free creatures to govern themselves freely. Still, in freely improvising our parts in the drama of our lives, we must plainly draw on the unique resources with which he endowed each of us. All this, too, has been rethought and reexpressed in secular analogues.

Religious persons imagine that the Creator is disappointed if we fail to live up to what we are capable of—at least as disappointed as we ourselves are likely to be. It is hard to hide such disappointment from ourselves if it is present, even if subconsciously. But secular persons, examining themselves as if from the viewpoint of an impartial spectator, may feel the same disappointment.

In our civilization, then, more secularized than it used to be, atheists and agnostics and those who are just not particularly religious (or tone-deaf regarding religion) are likely to have just as strong a sense of calling as religious persons, although they would not use the word *God*. After all, the God they don't believe in tends to be the God of Judaism, Christianity, and Islam, and the "self" they do know about is of the same cultural inheritance as that of believers. Though they are likely to speak of knowing themselves, finding their own identity, seeking their own fulfillment, even "doing their own thing," what they are doing is very like responding to a calling. Put more strongly, the secular language of self-knowledge, identity, self-fulfillment, and the pursuit of (personal) happiness has been so interblended with the traditional Jewish-Christian-Muslim sense of calling

for thousands of years that it is not easy to pull them apart. Within limits, all of us are talking about pretty much the same thing. We are probably flexible enough to try on each other's language and to translate from one to the other as needed.

METEORITES ACROSS THE SKY

People in business are not merely "rational economic agents." Each is also a human being in search of his calling. All are trying to live fulfilled lives, eager to mix their own identity with their work and their work with their identity. They want more satisfactions from work than money.

Further, people in business are not merely objects of analysis; they are subjects. They have other purposes in their economic activities than merely economic ones; they have other dimensions of their being to satisfy. More than that, they are ends in themselves. The soul of each of us is, in the words of the poet, "immortal diamond."

And the most important thing people wish to satisfy cannot be generalized because it is as unique to every person as an individual's DNA.

There is no more beautiful thing in the universe than the human person. What shows each of us to be distinctive is the trajectory of the calling we pursue, like meteorites across the night sky of history.

PART TWO
The Hurdles

Os Guinness is one of the best thinkers of our day. He is the amalgamated combination of philosopher, sociologist, and theologian, and he is blessed with the ability to write in an engaging and entertaining style.

The Call, published in 1998, is targeted to the popular audience—not an academic crowd. Although the book is not specifically written to the business community, it has terrific application to the arena of work. While it is common to see calling as something God uses when He's running low of pastors or missionaries to foreign countries, Guinness understands that the vast majority of people are called to "regular" jobs in the marketplace.

Guinness spent thirty years contemplating the concept of calling. "Calling is not what it is commonly thought to be," he writes. "It has to be dug out from under the rubble of ignorance and confusion. And, uncomfortably, it often flies directly in the face of our human inclinations. But nothing short of God's call can ground and fulfill the truest human desire for purpose."

The call is simple: "The truth that God calls us to himself so decisively that everything we are, everything we do, and everything we have is invested with a special devotion, dynamism, and direction lived out as a response to his summons and service."

Calling, as we pointed out in Part One, is foundational to an integrated life at work. So we easily could have included a selection from this book in that section. Instead, we chose to pull from one of the many practical chapters in *The Call*. In this chapter on "combating the noonday demon," Guinness makes the important connection between calling and work ethic.

Guinness postulates that calling is a sort of anti-sloth, a cure for the most misunderstood of the seven deadly sins. "[Sloth] is a condition of explicitly spiritual dejection that has given up on the pursuit of God, the true, the good, and the beautiful," Guinness writes.

Calling, therefore, is "the best antidote to the deadly sin of sloth." There are three points of entry for modern sloth (philosophical, cultural, and biographical), he points out, and calling runs counter to each of them. Thus, in answering our calling, we find the motivation to escape the temptation of slothfulness.

In this chapter, Guinness also adds to the discussion by examining the implications of sacred versus secular tensions of calling. We find that any system of ranking between different kinds of work, including between what is termed "sacred" and "secular" is a human invention and completely contrary to Scripture.

Guinness further clarifies this point when he writes, "The troublesome contradiction is not between secular and religious work but between work that is inspired by gifts and calling (whether secular or religious) and work that is directed solely by career."

4

Combating the Noonday Demon

from *The Call* by Os Guinness

"I would prefer not to." More than twenty-five times in little over as many pages Herman Melville's character repeats these five words, delivered politely but firmly, to bring America's most ambitious and energetic street to a standstill. "Bartleby the Scrivener: A Story of Wall Street," a short story published in 1853, no longer startles as it must have done its first readers in the nineteenth century. But its haunting central figure remains as unsettling as a modern homeless vagrant, and it brilliantly evokes the world of resigned forlornness and absurdity that such writers as Franz Kafka and Samuel Beckett have portrayed in our own century.

Melville's narrator is "a rather elderly man," an unambitious lawyer with chambers in Wall Street. He had done work, we are told, for robber-baron John Jacob Astor. From his youth upward he had been "filled with a profound conviction that the easiest way of life is the best." He was soon to meet his match. He already employed three people, two scriveners (or copyists of legal papers) and an errand boy known in the office by their nick-

names, Turkey, Nippers, and Ginger Nut. Gratified by his growing business, he advertised for a new scrivener and finds on his office threshold a figure "pallidly neat, pitiably respectable, incurably forlorn!"– Bartleby.

At first, Bartleby distinguishes himself by his industry. He did an extraordinary quantity of writing both by sunlight and by candlelight–"As if long famishing for something to copy, he seemed to gorge himself on my documents."

But then, on only his third day of work, when asked to help with some document checking, Bartleby confounds both his boss and his fellow-workers when "in a singularly mild, firm voice, [he] replied, 'I would prefer not to.'"

These words become Bartleby's five-word creed. Is the request politely repeated? "I would prefer not to," he replies. Does his boss insist? Is work put in front of his nose? Do the other workers ask him to assist them? "I would prefer not to," he intones. Is Bartleby asked to explain himself? Is he offered other jobs? Is he fired and told to find other work? Is he ordered to quit the premises once and for all?

Sometimes Bartleby doesn't answer at all; he stands in one of his profound "dead-wall reveries." More often he simply says, "I would prefer not to."

Naturally, Bartleby's noncompliance initially baffles and in the end infuriates his boss. In between, the narrator feels every emotion known to a caring employer and a decent human being. But nothing succeeds. Nothing gets through. The story rolls relentlessly toward its climax in "the Tombs," Manhattan's infamous nineteenth-century House of Detention. Bartleby, finally refusing even food, wastes away and dies, "his face towards a high wall."

What explains Bartleby's strange behavior? Is he "a little luny," as twelve-year-old Ginger Nut believes? Or fully deranged as the bystanders think? Is his noncompliance an intuitive political protest, a nineteenth-century precursor to Gandhian nonviolent resistance? Or is Bartleby, as modern critics have written, a case of "terminal *acedia*" (or sloth) at the heart of modern capitalism?

Melville leaves such questions like hooks buried in our minds and consciences. All he adds is "one little item of rumour" that the narrator heard a few months after the scrivener's death. Bartleby had come from Washington, D.C., where he had lost his job because of a change in administrations. He had been "a subordinate clerk in the Dead Letter Office" (for the storage and disposal of undeliverable mail).

"Dead letters!" Melville writes at the story's conclusion. "Does it not sound like dead men? Conceive a man by nature and misfortune prone to pallid hopelessness: can any business seem more fitted than that of continually handling those dead letters, and assorting them for the flames? . . . On errands of life, these letters speed to death. Ah Bartleby! Ah humanity!"

It is hard not to read something of Melville's own life into this story. When he was thirty-three he felt a failure. His great masterwork *Moby Dick,* published two years earlier in 1851, had sold only 2,300 copies and had been savaged by reviewers on both sides of the Atlantic. *Pierre,* published in 1832, sold only 2,030 copies over thirty-five years (earning over his lifetime the princely sum of $157). So as Melville complained in a letter in 1851 to his Massachusetts neighbor Nathaniel Hawthorne, "Dollars damn me." If sales are the public's letter to an author, Melville was not encouraged by his mail. He had tried to express in *Moby Dick,* he wrote, "the sane madness of vital truth," but the world was not interested.

Like Bartleby, Herman Melville felt his life had taken him down a blind alley and all he seemed to see was dead, blank walls. Or, as he wrote to Hawthorne, using the picture of a stagecoach changing horses while carrying mail (the theme of messages again): "Lord, when shall we be done changing? Ah, it's a long stage, and no inn in sight, and night coming, and the body cold."

BETTER BARBARISM THAN BOREDOM?

Whether "Bartleby the Scrivener" is read on its own or read against the backdrop of its author's life, it sharpens our appreciation of yet another aspect of the truth of calling—*calling is the best antidote to the deadly sin of sloth.*

Sloth, the fourth of the seven deadly sins, is today the most misunderstood of all—which is ironic because, properly understood, it is the characteristically modern sin. For a start, sloth must be distinguished from idling, a state of carefree lingering that can be admirable, as in friends lingering over a meal or lovers whiling away hours in delighted enjoyment. In W. H. Davies's famous lines, "What is this life, if full of care, / We have no time to stand and stare?" Or, as George Macdonald argued, "Work is not always required of a man. There is such a thing as sacred idleness, the cultivation of which is now fearfully neglected."

But sloth must also be distinguished from the modern notion of couch-potato lethargy ("Nearer my couch to thee," as *The New York Times* headlined it). Sloth is more than indolence and physical laziness. In fact, it can reveal itself in frenetic activism as easily as in lethargy because its roots are spiritual rather than physical. It is a condition of explicitly spiritual

dejection that has given up on the pursuit of God, the true, the good, and the beautiful. Sloth is inner despair at the worthwhileness of the worthwhile that finally slumps into an attitude of "Who cares?"

Defined in this way, it is plain, as Evelyn Waugh observed, that "sloth is not primarily the temptation of the young." It is what the medievals spoke of as "the noonday demon." It is a sluggishness of spirit, feeling, and mind that eventually overcomes the body like an after-lunch languor. A far cry from the early morning idealism and enthusiasms of youth, it is captured in such phrases as the listlessness of life, despondency over meaning, career doldrums, moral burnout, paralysis of will, and the expressive French words *ennui* and *anomie*.

There are three principal points of entry for modern sloth, overlapping at times but quite distinct, and calling runs counter to them all. The first is philosophical. Loss of faith in God, and therefore in eternity and immortality, leads inexorably to an erosion of vitality in life itself. Max Weber wrote of the secularizing of the modern world as "disenchantment." The magic and mystery of life viewed under the aspect of eternity is systematically reduced and destroyed. But C. S. Lewis wrote more aptly of our modern "enchantment," and Blaise Pascal wrote earlier still of the "incomprehensible spell" and "supernatural torpor" of the sloth that comes from loss of faith.

"One needs no great sublimity of soul," Pascal wrote in *Pensetes*, "to realize that in this life there is no true and solid satisfaction, that all our pleasures are mere vanity, that our afflictions are infinite, and finally that death which threatens us at every moment must in a few years infallibly face us with the inescapable and appalling alternative of being annihilated or wretched throughout eternity." Therefore, Pascal writes, "I make an absolute distinction between those who strive with all their might to learn and those who live without troubling themselves or thinking about it."

Pascal's warnings about the danger of indifference have been amply proved true in our century. Friedrich Nietszche may have written of the "death of God" with excitement ("We philosophers and 'free spirits' feel ourselves irradiated as by a new dawn by the report that the 'old God is dead'"). Bertrand Russell may have felt inspired by his atheistic vision of a "Free Man's Worship" ("Only on the firm foundation of unyielding despair can the soul's habitation henceforth be safely built"). But for countless modern people, the world without God and without faith is closer to Bartleby's dead-end passivity or to the murky alienation of Joseph K in Kafla's *Trial* and the forlorn pointlessness of Samuel Beckett's two tramps in *Waiting for Godot.*

The year after Beckett arrived in Paris, literary circles were rocked by the suicide of the writer Jacques Rigaut because it was such a contradiction of his earlier weariness: "There are no reasons for going on living, but no more are there any reasons for dying. . . . The only manner left us in which we can evidence our disdain for life is by accepting it. . . . Life is not worth the trouble of leaving it."

In his *Letters to Olga*, Václav Havel commented on the incidence of intelligent modern people who are cynical and have "lost faith in everything." Such "giving up on life," he said, is "one of the saddest forms of human downfall." But the important thing to note is that "it was not the evil of the world that ultimately led the person to give up, but rather his own resignation that led him to the theory about the evil of the world."

"The temptation of Nothingness," Havel mused, "is enormous and omnipresent, and it has more and more to rest its case on, more to appeal to. Against it, man stands alone, weak and poorly armed, his position worse than ever before in history." And then, in words reminiscent of Pascal, he concludes, "The tragedy of modern man is not that he knows less and less about the meaning of his own life, but that it bothers him less and less."

The second point of entry for sloth it cultural. We think of the rise of the modern world as the story of dynamism, energy, progress, and achievement—which it is. But we often overlook its other side. The world produced by such dynamism is a world of convenience, comfort, and consumerism. And when life is safe, easy, sanitized, climate-controlled, and plush, sloth is close.

The flipside of dynamic optimism is corrosive boredom. The couch potato is the half-brother of the astronaut. Equally the flipside of consumerism is complacency. The most compulsive of shoppers and channel-surfers move from feeling good to feeling nothing.

Soren Kierkegaard was a passionate earlier rebel against this modern sloth. "Let others complain that the age is wicked," he wrote of the mid-nineteenth century, "my complaint is that it is wretched, for it lacks passion. . . . Their lusts are dull and sluggish, their passions sleepy. They do their duty, these shop-keeping souls, but they clip the coin a trifle." Also in the nineteenth century, Charles Baudelaire wrote that "ennui, fruit of dreary apathy, takes on dimensions of everlastingness." And in a dark prophecy of modern boredom-bred violence and vandalism, Theophile Gautier wrote: "Better barbarism than boredom!"

The thought is arresting. Does the lethargy of sloth breed an itch for action, violence, and chaos? What is undeniable is that when comforts and convenience sap our energies and idealism, inactivity secretes sloth into our minds like a poison in the blood. Then, as lethargy, tedium, and futility overtake us, we progressively lower our ideals and succumb. The result, as Dorothy Sayers wrote devastatingly, is a slump into the sin of sloth—"the sin which believes in nothing, cares for nothing, seeks to know nothing, interferes with nothing, enjoys nothing, loves nothing, hates nothing, finds purpose in nothing, lives for nothing, and only remains alive because there is nothing to die for. We have known it far too well in the twentieth century," Sayers concluded. "The only thing perhaps that we have not known about it is that it is mortal sin."

When the Bible describes the occasion of King David's sin of adultery and then murder, it says revealingly, "In the spring, at the time when kings go off to war, David sent Joab out. . . ." Relaxed when he should have been on the job, inactive when he would normally be under arms, David was more than halfway open to temptation.

The third main entry point for sloth is biographical. There are natural points in our lives when each of us is especially prone to losing a sense of the worthwhileness of the worthwhile. Throughout history the most common moment is the experience of discouragement through failure. Today the most talked about is the pent-up frustrations of a "midlife crisis." Probably the worst of all is the combination of a midlife crisis that pivots on failure. Few things are more ignominious than failing at something that was not worth doing in the first place.

Midlife crises that are genuine and not simply fashionable are generally due to the tensions between three very different desires: for successful careers, for satisfying work, and for rich personal lives. Early in life the differences between our personal lives and our work may not be marked or obvious. But as life goes on, and especially if success in one sphere is not complemented by success in the other, a yawning chasm will open that leads to deep frustration. Sadly, studies show, a few people enjoy neither their work nor their personal lives; more enjoy their work but not their personal lives; only a few say they enjoy both.

Crises created by a contradiction between successful careers and satisfying work are even more fateful. For when we set out in youth and choose careers for external reasons—such as the lure of the salary, the prestige of the position, or pressure from parents and peers—we're setting ourselves up for frustration later in life if the work does not equally suit us for internal reasons, namely our giftedness and calling. "Success" may then flatter us on the outside as "significance" eludes us from the inside.

At that point many people jump to the opposite extreme where another frustration looms. They go wrong in thinking that "success" failed to satisfy because it was secular whereas "significance" will be fulfilling because it is religious. That is actually the "Catholics' distortion" again.

The troublesome contradiction is not between secular and religious work but between work that is inspired by gifts and calling (whether secular or religious) and work that is directed solely by career.

Any contradiction between our callings and our careers condemns us to be square pegs in round holes. But while the resulting midlife crisis may be severe, it may also serve as a wake-up call that turns out to be an opportunity as much as a crisis. Careers that express calling are as fulfilling as careers that contradict calling are frustrating.

The truth of calling addresses all these entry points of sloth. Personally summoned by the Creator of the universe, we are given a meaning in what we do that flames over every second and inch of our lives. Challenged, inspired, rebuked, and encouraged by God's call, we cannot for a moment settle down to the comfortable, the mediocre, the banal, and the boring. The call is always to the higher, the deeper, and the farther.

Awakened to our deepest gifts and aspirations, we know that consideration of calling always has to precede considerations of career and that we can seek the deepest satisfaction in work only within the perspectives of calling.

In short, every time the marsh gas of sloth rises from the swamps of modern life and threatens to overcome us, the call of God jerks us wide awake. Against the most sluggish temptation to feel "Who cares?" calling is the supreme motivation, the ultimate "why." God has called us, and we are never more ourselves than when we are fully stretched in answering. There is no yawning in response to this call.

Do you long to escape the smallness of a *life with no purpose higher than your own?* *To rise above the mediocrity, tedium, and* *quiet desperation of so many around you? To* *know a purpose no odds can daunt and no* *failure can dismay? Listen to Jesus of* *Nazareth; answer his call.*

Chuck Colson and Jack Eckerd come from different backgrounds. Colson rose to power as an attorney in the Nixon administration before going to jail for his part in the Watergate scandal; Eckerd founded and built one of the nation's largest drugstore chains. In time, however, they became friends who share strong convictions regarding the problems of America.

Colson, of course, had a much-publicized conversion to Christ, founded Prison Fellowship, and has become a respected critic of the culture through his radio program and his various books. Eckerd, who also has been involved in prison reform, understands work from the background of a businessman.

Together, they reached a simple conclusion: America has lost her work ethic.

In *Why America Doesn't Work,* Colson and Eckerd explain the intrinsic value of work and devote considerable attention to how we can address the lack of respect for work—a problem they say is at the core of many of society's problems.

The book was published in 1991 at a time when America's economic engine was "running down," so some may find their conclusions irrelevant in light of the economic boom that began shortly after the book was published. But the points they cover remain relevant, because America's success is rooted in more than mere economic prosperity. And economic success won't lead to cultural renewal unless people are willing to rediscover the benefits of meaningful work.

In the opening chapter, Eckerd and Colson use a trip they made to Russia to demonstrate where America is headed if she continues to reject the God-ordained institution of work. In 1990, the authors traveled to the Soviet Union to find a society that just didn't care about its work. The only place, in fact, where work seemed to matter was in the prisons, where work provided structure and meaning for the inmates.

"The hope, industry, and productivity that had disappeared from the streets of Moscow," they write, "seemed to be alive and well in the Soviet prisons."

Their observations validate our tenets of the purpose of work, reminding us that work was designed by God to fulfill needs of day-to-day personal significance (among other needs), not just fill our stomachs and pocketbooks.

Rather than celebrate the failings of socialism, the authors recognized a disturbing parallel between the Soviet Union of that day and where America was headed. This realization inspired them to pen *Why America Doesn't Work.* Their case for renewing a strong work ethic is valid regardless of a society's economic condition. Because valuing work, as they point out, creates something much bigger than economic success—it creates a culture that cares enough to take care of itself.

5

Something's Not Working

from *Why America Doesn't Work* by Charles Colson and Jack Eckerd

It is necessary to develop the people's sense of labor, and this has to be done as soon as possible because for half a century no one [in the USSR] has found any reward in work. There is no one to grow wheat for bread, no one to take care of cattle. Millions are living in conditions that cannot be called dwelling, and they spent decades in stinking hovels. The elderly and invalids are poor as beggars. Roads are in terrible condition, and nature itself is taking revenge.

—Aleksandr Solzhenitsyn

PERCHED ON THE BRINK of the twenty-first century, we look out across a land where our families are disintegrating, our streets have become drug-war combat zones, our classrooms are turning out thousands of functionally illiterate and morally bereft young people, our economy looks like it's on a roller-coaster, our government deliberately keeps millions idle, and our work force produces second-rate products while demanding first-rate benefits.

Things aren't working well here in America. The evidence is all around us. Too frequently, all you have to do is buy or use an American-made product.

Take the case of the missing wheel covers. Recently the Florida Highway Patrol added several top-of-the-line 1991 police cruisers to their fleets. These come equipped with powerful 350-cubic-inch V-8 engines, antilock brakes and "an annoying little problem." The plastic wheel covers keep falling off. So far the mystery hasn't been solved, since the covers seem to fly off—dangerous missiles hurtling through the air—at varying speeds. "We acknowledge that there is a problem with the wheel covers," said a company spokesman in a wonderful understatement. "The covers don't seem to have much endurance under adverse conditions."

Now certainly any manufacturer can occasionally end up with a defective product or encounter a glitch that must be ironed out of a certain production model, but this kind of "annoying little problem" has become all too familiar in our country. Something has happened to America's pride and workmanship, and because of it we are often being whipped in world trade.

In most consumer ratings, American products consistently slip behind foreign competitors, and a recent study concluded that in 1990 the United States, alone among the seven great industrial nations of the world, suffered an actual decline in its real standard of living.

Something is wrong.

Surveys reveal that fewer and fewer Americans want to work hard or take pride in what they do. Then there are the millions of citizens who don't—or won't work. Five million people live in permanently subsidized unemployment, while our welfare rolls continue to swell. Another million sit, bored and despairing, in overcrowded prisons, unable to contribute any economic support to either their families on the outside or to the bloated budgets required to support the prison system. And with all this, our crime rate is the highest in the free world.

The problem is so obvious that even a proudly liberal *New York Times* editorialist like Anna Quindlen acknowledges: "We are deeply dissatisfied with many of our social programs, if for no other reason than that they *do not work*. Education, welfare, crime have all come to seem like bottomless pits. Beneath them all is a black sea of poverty."

Something is *very* wrong.

Americans have had every advantage. North America possesses an abundance of natural resources and fertile land for agriculture. In the prenuclear age, two oceans insulated us from the turmoil of Asia and Europe. Conquering the frontier bred a hardy stock of ruggedly independent men and women who fashioned a democracy that depended on the industry of every citizen. These forebears passed down to us a heritage of industry, thrift, diligence, and respect for property known as the work ethic. Based on that ethic, the world's noblest experiment in political and religious freedom created an economic machine that for over a century has been the marvel of the world.

But the very thing that made America great is in trouble today. Our economic engine is running down. We are losing the work ethic.

Ironically, we had to travel to the other side of the globe to have this brought forcefully home to us.

In March 1990, the two of us went to the Soviet Union as part of an American delegation sent to visit five Soviet prisons, including Perm 35, the Siberian outpost where many of the most notorious dissidents have been held. Our purpose was twofold: to share expertise about prisons with Soviet officials, and to press for the release of political prisoners.

• • •

Every American enters the Soviet Union with conflicting emotions: excitement at passing through the once-impenetrable Iron Curtain and apprehension at what mysteries might lie beyond. We were no exception as our blue-and-white Aeroflot jetliner, with its winged hammer-and-sickle insignia, began its descent into Moscow's Shermetovo Airport. Our tension, however, also carried an edge of fear. Within hours, if all went well, we would go where few Westerners had gone before: the Soviet gulag.

Grim-faced soldiers patrolled the airfield, watching us closely as we left the plane and entered the terminal. A serious young man in uniform checked our passports and visas, then waved us through to gather up our luggage and deal with the stone-faced customs officers. To our great surprise and relief the contents of our baggage didn't get a second glance.

The only thing that gave the airport officials pause was our destination: when the customs officer noted that our visit included the city of Perm, he stared at us, rolled his eyes, and repeated the word "Perm" several times with an odd, almost smug smile, as if to say, "Do you know what you're getting into?"

The first real hitch in the journey seemed to be the car in which we were to be transported to Moscow; the driver couldn't get it started. He cranked the engine of the black Volga over and over until, with a great belch of smoke, it finally sputtered to life. With the vehicle creaking and shaking as though it might break apart at the next jolt, we rattled off toward the city over roads pocked with potholes large enough to swallow a Lada, the plagiarized Fiat that serves as the "people's car." While the machinery of communism had been breaking down, apparently so had everything else.

As we approached the city, we began to understand why Irina Ratushinskaya, the Soviet poet and heroic dissident, had entitled her memoirs *Grey Is the Color of Hope*.

The Moscow skyline was gray. The soot-covered buildings with their heavy Cyrillic lettering were gray. The snow on the ground was gray. The leaden, omnipresent war monuments were gray. The heavily polluted air was gray. Even the people on the streets were gray, unsmiling, weighed down. Only the crimson epaulets on the soldiers' uniforms and the blazes of gold on the onion domes of the Kremlin stood out in vivid and welcome contrast.

Because we arrived a day ahead of the rest of the delegation, we had to fend for ourselves for the first twenty-four hours, getting at least a glimpse of ordinary Soviet life before we were ushered into the showcase of Soviet officialdom. We were booked into a typical tourist hotel, the Intourist in downtown Moscow, a tall modern-looking building—at least it was modern on the outside. Inside, it was chaos and confusion. People charged around the enormous, smoke-filled lobby in all directions, babbling in a dozen languages, while a half-naked dancer attempted to lure customers into the hotel bar and swarms of prostitutes openly worked the crowd.

At the reception desk we produced our prepaid vouchers, only to be told they had only one room reserved.

"We have vouchers here for two rooms," we said.

"The computer shows that you have only one room. Your travel agency made a mistake."

We had prepaid and had the evidence to prove it, but obviously in the Soviet system the customer was never right. We ended up paying over again for a second room and were sent up to what the desk clerk called our "deluxe rooms."

When we got to our floor—in an elevator that stopped short of the doorway by four or five inches—we could only wonder at the desk clerk's definition of deluxe. Even the dim lighting could not disguise the partially painted plywood panel walls; the faded and frayed carpets; the seedy, broken-down sofas; and the corroded bathroom fixtures that dripped incessantly. The beds were clean enough, but everything was in disrepair.

Finding a place to eat proved even more frustrating than getting a place to sleep.

Soviet law dictates that all visitors use only Soviet currency. People can be detained for giving out American dollars, and the Soviets keep a careful check on this by having visitors list all of their currency when they arrive and again when they leave. As members of an official del-

egation we dared not violate these rules. The problem was, the hotel restaurants refused to accept rubles; they all wanted our illegal American dollars.

Just as we were getting desperate enough to check out the Moscow McDonald's that we had passed on our drive in from the airport, we encountered an American, an assistant producer of the "Columbo" television show, who was there on holiday.

When we mentioned our dilemma, the friendly young man remarked, "I've been here five days and I've only had two decent meals. And those were at McDonald's. It's the only place you can get served and get enough to eat." Even in the restaurants food was scarce, he said, and you often had to bribe the maitre d' to get a table, even in a half-empty dining room. After the black market, bribery was the biggest business in Moscow; everyone appeared to be on the take.

Our new acquaintance suggested we try the China Restaurant on the twentieth floor of the Intourist. "It's not great, but it's food," he said.

To this day we are uncertain what we ate that night—it was certainly not Chinese but at least the place accepted rubles, and we could fill up on bread.

Before we retired, we tried to make a phone call to let our State Department contact know we had arrived. However, in Moscow you can't let your fingers do the walking because the Soviets do not have phone books. As a result, it's virtually impossible to locate anyone's phone number, and there are no operators to help. We ended that first night in the Soviet Union feeling that nothing worked, and what was worse, nobody cared.

The next day, Sunday, we made the transfer from tourists to official delegates, and the contrast could not have been more dramatic. A KGB official whisked us away in a polished black limousine, took us to a fine restaurant for a sumptuous meal with one lavish course after another (the communist bureaucrats can miss just about anything but their meals and vodka), and moved us to an "official" hotel where the opulent lobby had walls inlaid with rich mahogany paneling and marble floors covered with Persian rugs—though even here the escalators were broken. Our rooms were elegant, with commodious, tiled bathrooms and polished brass fixtures.

On Monday morning a caravan of black limousines hauled our delegation and its attendant luminaries to Domodedovo, the largest airport in the Soviet Union, serving all cities east of Moscow. We arrived at the airport about 9:30 and were told our flight would leave at 10:30.

At 10:40 they said, "Departure will be a bit late."

The plane finally took off at 1:30. Three hours later we landed in Perm.

The Ural Mountains form the boundary between the plains of European Russia and Asian Siberia, and just west of the spine of the Urals lies the industrial city of Perm. The capital of Oblensk, this city of 1.5 million people is a place of paralyzing drabness, several shades grayer than Moscow.

During the next day and a half we visited Perm 29, a traditional prison housing ordinary offenders, and Perm 35.

Certain names evoke powerful images and come to convey almost universal, generic meaning. Waterloo is synonymous with defeat, Benedict Arnold with betrayal, and gulag immediately conjures up oppression and "man's inhumanity to man." Perm Camp 35 is the crown jewel of the gulag.

Traveling over washed-out, sometimes flooded roads—evidence of the fact that it is still impossible to cross the USSR on a paved road—the bleak Siberian landscape fulfilled our every expectation. The late March winds chilled our bodies, and the sight of rough-strung barbed wire and guard towers bristling with guns made us uneasy.

Guards led us through huge gates and along a maze of pathways cut into the mountains of snow to a string of one- and two-story frame buildings that looked as though they dated back to the days of the czars.

Inside there was fresh paint everywhere, and everything appeared freshly scrubbed. Drab doors and walls had been hastily daubed with garish blue and green paint; in their zeal, they had even painted the floors.

Colonel Nikolai Osin, commandant at Perm 35 since 1972 and a man whose unfeeling eyes reflected equal contempt for visitors and inmates, herded us into a conference room where we were to interview several of the prisoners. Against three walls they had arranged chairs for the Soviet officials and our delegation; against the fourth wall sat a chair facing a television camera and glaring lights.

We protested this intimidating arrangement, but Osin was adamant. "It is the law," he insisted, wielding absolute authority over his sixty-one-acre kingdom.

With this arrangement, these men won't be able to tell us a thing, we thought. But they did. While the KGB camera recorded their every word and expression, six of the most celebrated political prisoners in the world boldly told us the truth about the charges trumped up against them, how they had been denied their rights and had their visiting privileges canceled. At times they smiled almost defiantly at their captors as they sat in that lonely chair and exposed the horrors of the gulag. Some had spent as many as fifteen years in this brutal outpost. They spoke of lengthy solitary confinement for minor violations; one had been in solitary five times, while another had been kept there for twelve months. All complained that their mail had been tampered with and even blocked. At the end of the interview each

thanked us and marched out of the room, shoulders squared, head high.

Aleksander Goldovitch, a physicist and an outspoken Christian, charged with treason for trying to row a rubber raft across the Black Sea to Turkey, asserted that they were prisoners of conscience. Later in his cold, cavelike, concrete cell he proudly pointed to a small cross he had etched in the cement above the door, a symbol of that faith which sustained him.

The Soviet system had done everything imaginable to beat these men into submission. Yet somehow in this hopeless outpost where one might expect to find a bleak, frozen winter of the spirit, these prisoners had kept their sense of individual dignity and purpose.

An amazing paradox.

We spent the remainder of our time back in Moscow, where we visited three more prisons, including the women's prison in Mozhaisk, a sprawling complex of brick and frame buildings holding nine hundred women convicted of offenses ranging from shoplifting to murder. Although conditions were austere, the officials boasted about such innovations as conjugal visits, furloughs, and release policies for pregnant women. They eagerly showed us their theater, education rooms, a well-stocked library with shiny, new leather-bound Bibles, and the mess hall.

We arrived at the mess hall just as lunch was being served. Some inmates were still passing through the line, having their trays filled; most were seated at long bench-style tables. Except for an occasional sideways glance, no one looked at us. Heads down, they kept eating.

Never one to be intimidated, Jack walked up to the line of women and asked casually, "How's the food?"

Oh, no! thought Chuck. *Now we're going to have to try this stuff.*

Sure enough, the commandant invited us to eat, and although the stew being slopped on the trays looked less than appetizing, we got in line. As we took our trays and sat at one of the tables and began to eat, the mood in the room changed dramatically. Women lifted their heads and looked at us; they began to point and chatter. One got up from her place and came over and sat next to us. She spoke excellent English, and as we chatted, others gathered around. One woman beamed widely, repeatedly pointing to a cross around her neck.

What amazed us in Mozhaisk, as in the other Soviet prisons we visited, was the fact that work seemed to be the heart of prison life. Every inmate had a job, six days a week, eight hours a day, and their production lines hummed with efficiency. At Perm we had seen most of the prisoners hard at work in various machine shops, where each had a production quota. With the money they earned they paid the cost of their confinement. At Mozhaisk we found a garment factory, where we spoke with a number of the women who were cutting and trimming fabric or running sewing machines. They appeared alert, interested in their work, some of them almost cheerful. Prison officials can disguise a lot of things with institutional whitewash, but not attitudes, and it was evident that morale was high in this place.

Each woman had a quota of four hundred pieces a day, for which she was paid 180 rubles a month, approximately two-thirds the average wage of a Soviet worker on the outside. The women told us that they were allowed to save money for their release or send it home. If they produced 10 percent more than their quota, they earned a bonus. Most worked overtime to do this. Could this be the initial signs of free enterprise?

No one knows the brutality of the Soviet prison system better than Aleksandr Solzhenitsyn, Nobel-Prize-winning writer and dissident who endured ten years in the gulag, often surviving on bare subsistence gruel while forced into hard labor in the frozen Siberian tundra. During his imprisonment he composed what would become *One Day in the Life of Ivan Denisovich*. In the classic novel, Solzhenitsyn recounts how backbreaking manual labor gave his life purpose. Even with his body stretched to the breaking point, he could feel a stab of pride when a gulag official looked over the rows of bricks he had laid and commended, "Good line."

Irina Ratushinskaya, the Soviet poet whose writings were pronounced subversive because they spoke of God and freedom, detailed her own gulag experience in her memoirs. In that bleak existence, full of deprivation and misery, her prison job making gloves provided a sense of purpose, occupied her mind, and gave meaning to her otherwise empty days.

Before we left the Soviet Union—a moment most visitors look forward to as much, or more, than their arrival—we walked the streets of Moscow and visited several stores. There we saw empty shelves and unsmiling people waiting in long lines for hours to buy the few products available. In a supermarket half the shelves were bare, and customers were lined up to buy small bags of vegetables and scrawny chickens. We saw no fruit of any kind and were told that everything was rationed, including sugar, salt, and even soap.

Then our KGB escort drove us to the airport, bypassed the long lines at the ticket counters, and ushered us into a plush VIP lounge filled with top party and government officials.

"The hostess will escort you directly to your plane," he said, and with a half bow handed us our papers and passports.

While we waited for our flight, we sipped lemonade and nibbled from trays of caviar canapes, offered at ludicrously low prices. As we sat there talking, a well-dressed man stepped up and leaned against the counter next to us. He took a piece of paper from his pocket and began to read from it. As he did so, the waitress produced a bag of twelve lemons—as plump and juicy as any we'd ever seen in Florida's citrus groves—two huge eclairs dripping with thick chocolate, a large bag of cookies, and two one-pound bags of candy. The man lined the goods up on the counter, checking off his shopping list, then handed the waitress a fifty ruble note—approximately eight dollars at the then official exchange rate but only two dollars on the black market.

Surely he can't buy all this for that amount, we thought.

Then we got an even greater shock. The waitress handed him thirty-five rubles in change!

This party member had just spent a trifling sum for a haul he could sell at an enormous profit on the booming Moscow black market, or he could stock the shelves of his *dacha,* the country estates made available to the ruling bureaucrats. While the ordinary citizens struggled for the barest essentials of life, government officials like this man— approximately five million of them—were living in the very best apartments, eating at their lavish restaurants, and shopping at their own well-stocked stores where the prices have not been raised in decades!

On the plane we leaned back in our seats almost in stunned silence, reflecting on our recent experiences.

What we had seen was not only the collapse of socialism, but a society sick at heart. A society where the citizens walked the streets dejected and despairing. A society where hotel clerks and waiters didn't care whether they served you or had to be bribed to do so. A society riddled with crime and where suicide has become an increasing avenue of escape. A society where the black market is the only economy that works. We had seen a society suffering from the advanced stages of what the Danish philosopher Soren Kierkegaard called "soul sickness."

Then the irony hit us! For juxtaposed against all this were the images of the smiling, confident, determined men and women we had met behind the grim prison walls. The hope, industry, and productivity that had disappeared from the streets of Moscow seemed to be alive and well in the Soviet prisons.

It would have been natural for us to gloat over what we had seen. After all, we were both lifelong anticommunists, and Jack had been in the midst of an exciting free market economy that boomed in the fifties and sixties. Now, with the Soviet economy crumbling fast and the country's spirit sapped, the world was seeing the bankruptcy of socialism. The Soviet colossus was collapsing, and democracy, the free market, and capitalism had deservedly won the day.

But the disquieting parallels restrained us.

Weren't we seeing some of these same signs in America? Oh, to be sure, nothing like Moscow, but signs nonetheless—and troubling ones: workers producing and caring less; American-made products of poorer and poorer quality losing out in world markets; a growing privileged class; the spread between workers' and managements' salaries growing wider; rising crime and a deadly, entrenched welfare state.

As our plane touched down on American soil, we were grateful to be home, grateful to be Americans, but we also began to wonder whether we'd just seen a glimpse of our own future if we squander our heritage.

Laura Nash is the director of the Institute for Values-Centered Leadership at Harvard Divinity School. In the early 1990s, however, she was a professor at Harvard Business School who had been reared in what she called a "Protestant Congregational tradition." At that time, she knew plenty about business but not much about evangelicals. Who better, then, to do a study of evangelical CEOs?

"It is important to keep in mind that the questions that initially led me to do a study of evangelicals were much larger than evangelicalism itself," she writes in *Believers in Business*. "I was hoping to gain insight into how people who were completely committed to living a Christian life and who were successful in business approached their responsibility at work whatever their denomination."

This was no easy task. But Nash's background made her sensitive to spiritual beliefs and the importance of those beliefs to people in their everyday lives. And she was enough of an outsider that her work was taken seriously by peers who weren't part of the evangelical community. The result was a first-of-its-kind study on faith and work.

Nash interviewed eighty-five evangelical CEOs (all men), who "a) were admired as being faithful Christians, b) had achieved success in their businesses, and c) were willing to talk with me." As she interviewed them, she began to see some themes in the regular critical conflicts between the business culture and their faith.

Those conflicts were boiled into "seven tension" – things like the love for God versus the pursuit of profit. She also identifies three typical personal responses to those tensions.

"The first of two types of evangelicals, whom I call the *generalists* and the *justifiers,* are characterized by their denial of conflicting impulses," she writes. "These two groups either ignore or rationalize potential discrepancies between 'business as usual' and Christian ethics.

"The third type of evangelical, whom I call the *seeker,* has a more complicated response. Rather than seeing business and Christianity as automatically compatible, the seekers find that faith does two things simultaneously: *It demands an awareness* of conflicting values, while it also *becomes the mediating factor* in the ongoing tensions between the must of religion and the must of business."

In this chapter, Nash explains how she came up with the seven creative tensions and what they tell us about the people who face them. Using the tensions as an organizing framework, Nash provides insights into how faith continually reshapes the attitudes of evangelical CEOs and, thus, helps them deal with the challenges of leading people and running a business.

When exploring the different responses to these tensions—the generalist, the justifier, and the seeker—Nash makes the case that the seeker provides the best example of active faith. It's both a result of her research and a challenge for those who desire to have an active faith. And it shows that while her understanding of evangelicals may have been limited at the start of the project, she grew into an expert on her topic by the time it was completed.

6

Common Tensions Believers Face

from *Believers in Business* by Laura Nash

> They do not understand
> that it is by being at variance
> with itself that life
> coheres with itself: a
> backward-stretching harmony,
> as of a bow or a lyre.
>
> —Heraclitus

I AM TRAVELING on a plane. The person next to me asks me about my work. I tell him I am writing a book on evangelical CEOs. I might as well say I'm working on ancient forms of sexual perversion, to judge from the curious mix of contempt and fascination with which this information is usually greeted.

I have it on good authority after three years of extensive business travel and casual conversations that evangelical businesspeople are assumed by nonevangelicals to fall into one of three categories, depending on the person offering the judgment:

• They are sleazebags who calculatingly use Jesus' name to grease their hypocritical smiles and line their pockets.

• They are rigid, uptight neo-Nazis who exploit friendship to "sell" Jesus and who have no idea of their own destructiveness.

• (This last generalization is usually voiced in a confessional tone of surprise.) They are discovered to be decent, hardworking human beings—in *spite* of their religion.

An example of the last characterization came from a fellow passenger on the Delta shuttle between Boston and New York:

> You know, my boss is evangelical. It really surprised me. He's amazing. I really respect him. He always has time for people. He knows the personal life of everyone in the company. Always asking people about their family, their

boyfriends. And he's always calm. You know, when everyone else is panicking, he'll just smile and calm us down, and figure out a way to get the business. And he's very straight [that is, conservative]. He works very hard—no one works harder—but he doesn't seem "owned" by the business.

Evangelicals come in various forms and sizes, and the impressions they make on others vary dramatically. At the risk of generalizing, we know that everyone has met the snake-oil salesman whose invocations of Jesus are about as genuine as a tin dime; most people have been scared off by the rigidity of some evangelicals, whose uptightness *must* be hiding something that is no good for everyone else; and some people have met the plausible evangelicals, whose decency and intellect fall into the "normal" range of human behavior. Casting such differences into rigid typologies has little point and would be morally distasteful.

Nevertheless, the fact that there were certain general traits commonly shared by the CEOs I interviewed suggested that I could appropriately make some sort of qualified generalization about their business mind-set. Making such a generalization also seemed to be a helpful way of moving beyond the knee jerk reactions that make up the popular characterization of the evangelical business leader.

To be sure, the group that I interviewed

generally emphasized industriousness and a methodical, rational approach to life and business. On the whole, though with notable exceptions, these business leaders were relatively modest in lifestyle. But while they may have been appalled at a Charles Keating-type three-thousand-dollar lunch for five at Le Cirque, they were also not John Calvins in modern dress. They were neither totally unmaterialistic nor against leisure time. As I noted earlier, some of those I surveyed were surprisingly modest in their choice of cars or houses, but many others lived in extremely upscale communities and had large yachts, fancy cars, and expensive leisure-time lifestyles.

It is not on the issues of materialism, industriousness, or worldliness that the evangelical CEO can be definitively called distinctive. On these grounds they exhibit about the same work values as an ambitious, rational workaholic whom you could find in many secular, not-so-humanistic business circles. The difference showed itself most obviously in terms of the personal style that interviewees exhibited *as CEOs*. The "typical" participant was a soft-spoken person, intimate in manner, more like a minister or old-time professor than a J. R. Ewing. His descriptions about his company tended to favor the small incident rather than the bigger picture—even if his firm was in the Fortune 500 and doing millions or billions of dollars of business a year. His choice of issues in connection with a question about conscience or business ethics was usually about a counseling encounter with a secretary or an hourly employee rather than, say, about environmental policy, product safety, or lobbying for economic policy with other business leaders.

The typical participant carried the personal element to the discussion of business, mentioning his own home life or the sexual habits of employees in what was purportedly a discussion of business philosophy and faith. He took a holistic view of problems, with the result that a discussion about a choice of product was sometimes abruptly punctuated with a story about a family problem. The two topics were reconciled, however, by the belief that it is the spiritual health of the inner, private person that will ultimately determine the moral and practical health of any business problem. There was a fundamental self-confidence to the evangelical that on the surface raised him above being personally agitated by the "little" things of life, however high the financial stakes. He was not your frenetic mover and shaker. He was calm.

This is a portrait of what could be called a domesticated capitalist. He is domesticated not only in the sense that he seeks to tame the more bestial side of modern capitalism (such as Wall Street predators on the hostile takeover scene), but literally domesticated in terms of his household concerns—marriage, child rearing, friendship, and family participation in a religious community—which extends even to the way he understands and arranges his business career. Not one participant failed to mention some important aspect of his home life (satisfactory or otherwise) and of his prayer or other spiritual activities. A good many, however, never got around to describing their product choices, the ethics of the industry in which they operate, or even a specific economic decision.

The personal "style" of the evangelical CEOs who are described in this book may be familiar to the reader, but it does not conform to the general public's expectations about the personal qualities needed for success in business today. A joint study by Korn/Ferry International and Columbia Business School of senior executive views on leadership in the next century revealed that the very characteristics that the participants in my study exhibited were rated *lowest* in terms of potential leadership. (The precise attributes were *"tough, personable, patient, dignified, and conservative."*) As that report notes, most of these characteristics are "old-fashioned" values: "They describe the CEO who ushered in the 20th century."

Despite popular opinion to the contrary, the group interviewed for this book represents substantial business success and challenges us to reconsider some of the critical assumptions being made today about the nature of successful business leadership. Whether or not we accept the sincerity or spiritual correctness of these evangelicals, or their general Norman Rockwell style, we *do* need to carefully consider and analyze their effectiveness in the marketplace and the health of their organizations. *The portrait presented in this book is an attempt to test (and hopefully explode) some of the more thoughtless stereotypes held by nonevangelicals and evangelicals alike.*

Briefly, I will show that the successful impact of evangelical faith on business management is best understood as a series of sustained tensions—seven in all—that describe the recurrent issues identified by participants. The running theme throughout this analysis is *contrast*. Evangelicalism, with its focus on the spiritual, the relational, the domestic, and the holistic, poses certain contrasts with the traditional requirements of a large, capitalistic organization. Strong investment ratings do not automatically coincide with people needs inside a company. Competitive pressures do not instantly lend themselves to an attitude of loving one's neighbor. And the pluralistic agnosticism of today's workplace rarely welcomes the mention of Jesus or any other kind of witnessing.

How then does such a faith play a role in this world? Is that role good or bad for business? More to the point, what *kind* of business values are we talking about?

What sort of competitive characteristics emerge from participants' visions of good business practices?

As the interviewees probed their own attitudes toward work, career, business success, and spiritual well-being, certain common beliefs about management and Christianity were expressed so often that they suggested a group of core concepts that seem to drive evangelical business thinking. In the pages that follow, I have organized these recurring themes around seven basic tension points:

1. The love for God
   and the pursuit of profit
2. Love and the competitive drive
3. People needs and profit obligations
4. Humility and the ego of success
5. Family and work
6. Charity and wealth
7. Faithful witness in the secular city

As you can see, the first part of each "tension" describes an important Christian theme, while the second half describes some basic components of business enterprise.

Although all but the seventh tension represent familiar issues of conscience to any enlightened businessperson, these particular seven also betray an evangelical slant that is evident by what is not included. Absent here are the larger organizational perspectives—global problems such as overseas bribery, or grand schemes for economic development. Instead, as I have already noted, the interviewees tended to describe their business values in terms of relational or domestic problems—a negotiation with a customer, a small incident with a secretary, a marriage problem triggered by business events, or a situation with an unethical employee—rather than larger-scale political or ethical concerns. In seeking to analyze the role of faith in business, these believers in business, as I came to call them, tended to start with their own behavior rather than with the behavior of others.

What the Seven Tensions Explain

The expression of themes in the form of the seven tensions is somewhat artificial, in that no one specifically identified seven, six, or even one "tension" to represent his business philosophy. And yet the problems these men described, their occasions for prayer, and their understanding of what it takes to be a business success, proved to hinge on these same seven oppositions time and again. Though I did not originally pose these seven as the basis for discussion, they summarize the most frequently mentioned themes in the interviews. They also provide a useful basis for others to explore the role of faith in their own business lives or that of their spouse.

I seized upon the idea of these seven

tensions almost by accident. In many cases I found my interviewees making statements that on the surface appeared to be contradictory, and yet I was reluctant, in taking their entire interviews into account, to pass these things off as mere "denial" or hypocrisy.

For example, a CEO might state categorically within five minutes that (1) "Money is nothing—it is God who counts," and (2) "Profit is very important, critical to business." Or a question about business responsibility would often prompt the CEO to offer a series of non-business examples. By giving such examples, he seemed to imply that the economic and practical concerns of business are inconsequential.

The problem was that the participants were men of good standing in both fields. How would I explain that they were regarded as men of faith and that they were demonstrably good businessmen? There were too many participants for me to attribute their business success wholly to chance, and there were too many concretely faith-oriented examples for me to assume that their faith meant nothing in a business context. These men wholly supported a capitalistic system in theory, and at the same time described a set of religious-cultural values that on the surface, at least, were in discord with the basic elements of capitalism.

What was going on here? Was I encountering the world's greatest collection of hypocrites? Or was it something at once more profound and less derogatory?

When the interviewees were confronted with the suggestion that business as they described it posed certain inevitable contradictions of Christian doctrine, many of them sidestepped the issue.

There are two likely but contradictory explanations for this phenomenon. One explanation is that the evangelical CEO has failed to assimilate spiritual concerns into his business activities. Wittingly (in which case it would be hypocrisy) or unwittingly (in which case the source would be some form of intellectual failure or psychological denial), he has not achieved the kind of worldly relevance of faith to which he aspires. The alternative explanation is that an assimilation of faith does indeed occur but is so successful that it is impossible for the CEO to distinguish the pieces anymore.

I, for one, am quite reluctant to pass judgment on people's sincerity. I do not have perfect pitch when confronted with the music of the soul. Nor do many other people I know. Most judgments of religious or ethical hypocrisy rest on serious misperceptions about human fallibility and nonconformity.

Evangelical stereotypes are no exception. It is assumed that every perceived imperfection or ambiguity of character in a self-avowed Christian must be self-serving and therefore unchristian and therefore hypocritical. Short of choosing

martyrdom or self-imposed poverty, which are also capable of provoking a cynical interpretation, the Christian business person hasn't got a chance of obtaining spiritual success, according to the public.

By assuming that the fundamentals of economic success are essentially negatives on one's Christian scorecard we fail to address the very affirmative connection that these men see between their careers and their faith. As long as the standing question remains quantitative—that is, How "Christian" is such and such a practice?— resolution is difficult. However, the assumption that there is an automatic complementarity between Christianity and the needs of business flies in the face of the real-world experience of an unforgiving marketplace of shareholders who are in it for the short term.

But if we start with the notion that there are indeed inherent, recurrent tensions between Christianity and business practice in a capitalistic system, we can rephrase the operating question to a qualitative one: How does faith (in this case, evangelical faith) play a role in these contradictory claims on the Christian? This question is the more effective one. First, it faces up to real problems of business behavior among Christians and nonchristians. Second, it admits the concept of the paradox—that is, an apparent contradiction that is nonetheless true.

I concluded that the only way to understand the interviews without shortchanging the real struggles of conscience these men have faced was to recast the remarks of the CEOs in the form of a series of sustained tensions. The ways in which the CEOs responded to specific examples of these tensions varied dramatically, as you will soon see from the character types I have outlined. But the most compelling examples occurred when the participant sustained and transformed the tensions into a *creative paradox,* reflecting the paradoxical nature of Christian spiritual claims and the worldly concerns of profit making.

THREE CATEGORIES OF RESPONSES

Such tensions could be, and frequently are, seen as mutually exclusive by evangelicals and nonevangelicals alike. They can be seen as the ultimate weapon, striking a fatal blow to capitalism from a Christian standpoint, or a fatal blow to Christianity from a business standpoint.

I found a real resistance to the idea of tension itself in many of those I interviewed. Interviewees tended to fall into three basic categories, determined by personality style, intellectual sophistication, theological assumptions, and psychological bias. As I mentioned in the preface, I have named these categories the generalist, the justifier, and the seeker. *The third type—the seeker—is of the greatest interest in this book and, I believe, provides the best*

example of active faith. It should be said that a Seeker approach was by far the most frequent among this group of interviewees.

The Generalist and the Justifier

The first type, the *generalist,* never gets down to specific examples from the right-hand, or business, side of the stated tensions. No matter how hard he is pressed, he manages to evade the suggestion that determining the right thing to do from a Christian's standpoint can be difficult or contrary to common practice. A common conviction among the generalists is that there is never a real problem in their own lives between faith and the requirements of the business. Given specific, obvious inconsistencies between an ethic built on honesty and love and, say, an apparently deceptive business practice in his own firm, he might acknowledge the inconsistencies as a problem but would then change the subject back to a reaffirmation of faith rather than discuss the dilemma.

Let's suppose that his company has launched an advertising campaign based on wildly exploitative gender stereotypes. When asked to explain it, the generalist might reply that he "sees no problem with the ad." He has never really had any problems knowing what was right. He will then quickly shift his focus to the general importance of home life and parenting as the real source of values, moving on from there to affirmative examples of times at home that strengthened his own or his children's relationship to Jesus. As one participant commented, "Doing everything according to your faith is not about how it comes out in the wash. As long as your motives are pure, you're okay."

The second type, the *justifier*, is very comfortable with the basic idea that the right-hand sides of the seven tension equations, which typify economic concerns, are supported by the Bible. What he does not do is demonstrate how specific biblical injunctions apply to such sticky problems as a hostile takeover or a boss who is unethical or a below-standard wage rate for first-line employees. The justifier tends to see his own economic success as the justification of his faith. For example, if he has preceded his decisions with prayer, asking God to help him "win" a deal, it seems apparent to him that his desire to win is consistent with God's will in that he wins over and over again. Capitalism must be godly. Any suggestion of tension between his desire to win each deal and other requirements of his faith (such as to serve others) is overshadowed by his strong (and often genuine) demonstration of a charitable and sensitive *attitude* in nearly any business decision. Said one CEO, who was unable to specify any of his remarks:

It's not about what you do; it's about your attitude. Get that right and the rest follows. If you love God, that's all that counts. The most important thing is to make sure your perspective is correct: who you serve.

Another CEO commented:

I feel a call to do the best I can do with what I can do, with the God-given talents I have. . . . In business I have to worry about a return on every investment. But I don't see it as a double standard, but rather different degrees of latitude.

So it is not surprising to find that the justifier's choice of examples is either about very obvious cases of law breaking and getting caught or about decisions that were unfailingly admirable: special attention to a secretary, meticulous honesty during a negotiation, charitable deeds in the local community. Most of these examples are supported by an argument of enlightened self-interest. That is, if you do the right thing in business, you will do well economically; if you do the wrong thing, you will be punished by the marketplace. A comment by one businessman from Boston is a good illustration:

I have a hard time thinking of illustrations simply because business is trying to find people we can help. That requires confidence, and if they thought you were a liar and a cheat, they wouldn't even let you in the door.

When asked how a Christian should handle a situation where his boss is lying and cheating, the same man replied with another justifying scenario: "Those people don't last in business."

More entrenched tensions, such as when it is permissible to "bend" the truth, or how many days should be spent away from the family for the sake of the business, are glossed over much as in the generalist's remarks. Unlike the generalist, the justifier tends to acknowledge that both sides of the tension equation are important to him, but he resists the idea of their being contradictory, recalling only the occasions when business instinct and Christian paradigms seem complementary.

For example, when I asked one particularly self-satisfied businessman if there were any dangers that a young Christian should avoid in the marketplace, he laughingly replied, "You shouldn't run prostitution rings in the city." His implication was that all the issues were already obvious to any good Christian. I tried again. "That's it?" I asked with seeming incredulity. He replied evenly:

"I would say there's very little that's not okay, as long as you keep in mind Christian principles. I mean, you can be a bartender. But you shouldn't be involved in the underworld or do anything illegal."

Essentially, these first two types—the generalist and the justifier—attempt to deal with conflict by denying its exist-

ence. They simply cannot imagine, no matter how hard they are pressed, a really problematic test of their faith. The generalist does this by never linking his understanding of Christian ethics (which is dominated by issues of sexuality and one's personal relationship with God) and management in the same set of problems. One wonders at times if there is any business decision that would agitate his conscience as much as one hint of illicit flirting. The justifier limits his examples to happy complementarities and ignores the more bothersome aspects of business.

Some of their denial is surely an attempt to put as favorable a light on evangelicalism as possible. They do not want outsiders to get the wrong impression by calling their attention to ethical lapses among the brethren. Others seem to have a theologically naive fear that the very suggestion of conflict between religion and business somehow contradicts a strong personal faith. If the sign of a first-class intelligence is to hold two opposing ideas at once, the justifier and the generalist flunk a basic theological IQ test. To them the admission of a possible dilemma is tantamount to a confession of spiritual doubt. Better to look the other way.

This strong tendency toward denial is a chief reason, in my opinion, why evangelicals are regarded by outsiders with suspicion or misunderstanding. It is very easy to assume that the glossy facade, the unfailing beatific smile all the way to the bank, hides a deep-seated hypocrisy. Evangelicals themselves regard some of their brothers and sisters in this light. As one evangelical CEO told me, "Some of the believers in my workplace are the last ones I'd trust."

But while hypocrisy explains some instances of denial, it did not generally seem to characterize the group of CEOs I interviewed. None of them were involved in the kinds of public scandals that would logically result from really venal cynicism—the kind of hypocrisy that was displayed in the savings and loan crisis, for example. Indeed, one CEO was in the personally difficult position of cooperating with the federal government in building a case against his chairman (also an evangelical), who had squandered a local S&L's assets. The CEO's condemnation of such behavior was unequivocal; but like a true seeker, he also found it very difficult to know how to give Christian love to the boss while essentially contributing to the government's case against the man.

But even if we absolve the generalist and justifier of deliberate concealment or hypocrisy, there is nonetheless a serious problem with their approach in terms of providing models of evangelical leadership from a spiritual and business standpoint.

Both the justifier and the generalizer, even when they are well-intentioned, decent people, fail to articulate any *public* meaning to the Christian's life, including his or her business life. Rather, they

exhibit a faith that corresponds to Peter Berger's description of a wholly privatized religion: religious relevance is restricted to one's "inner space," domestic activities, or individual personality traits such as being "nice." This sort of compartmentalization of the sacred and the secular is unsatisfactory to evangelicals because of the holistic orientation of their faith. And so they develop avoidance mechanisms for concealing the privatization of their religion.

And yet the conflicts with faith are there. In most cases, economic success does not come without placing the evangelical worldview and ethic in some jeopardy. Even a simple biblical directive such as not working on the Sabbath is nearly impossible to maintain by an executive in a large firm. In fact, several men said that they drew the line at working on the Sabbath, but when pressed they admitted that they would travel on the Sabbath to get to a Monday morning meeting. There are many such examples of the conflict between faith and the business culture, and between profit obligations and Christian commitments.

These points of conflict are frequently what I call "Siamese twin" problems. Two things are linked together in a way that cannot be maintained. One twin must be sacrificed for the other to live. Such a choice is unthinkable but inescapable. If nothing is done, if you turn your back, both will die.

The evangelical businessperson is constantly confronted with such choices. Should he or she invest in a very good health plan for employees or in product development to ensure jobs down the road? Should the evangelical travel on the Sabbath and get the business or attend the Bible study class on Sunday evening? There is no way to justify "turning one's back" or to expect capitalism to offer an automatic solution that will reward both one's faith and one's business expectations. Nonetheless, a generalist or justifier may not notice that he or she is not facing up to the problem because they have constructed elaborate "blinders" based in part on the strength of their religious belief. What is more, for the most part there is no "ethics doctor" to spell out these choices in inescapable terms. Mature people do this for themselves.

The Seeker

I discovered, however, that many business leaders were, in fact, acutely aware of these dilemmas and prepared to address them. I have called this third type of evangelical business leader the *seeker*, because he is willing to struggle with difficult choices in order to best serve his faith. The seeker, on whom the concept of the seven creative tensions is based, does not try to eliminate a suggestion of conflict between the requirements of the business and what his faith calls him to do or to feel.

Nor does he regard the tensions that most people feel between the promptings of a generous heart and a hardheaded economist as mere trade-offs (the positives and negatives on one's Christian scorecard). As former Eastman Gelatine president Frank Butler remarked:

> Conflict is a part of life. It's naive to expect that your faith will help you find one final solution to problems. But faith tells you the right way to deal with conflicts.

Of the three types of evangelical business leaders, the seeker takes the most dynamic view of the tensions between Christian belief, human failing, and economic practicality. He confronts these tensions, and through prayer and the perspective of faith, seeks out a course of action consistent with Christianity. *Faith itself becomes the mediating factor* in these tensions.

Another reason that I call this type of leader the seeker is that the process of his business thinking is as important as the actual deed. He genuinely wrestles with his Christian conscience and business responsibilities in order to seek out as compatible a response as possible, even though he knows that the concept of being a "perfect" Christian doing the perfect Christian deed is beyond any human's comprehension.

In many cases, however, his seeking leads to the creation of third alternatives that are more in line with biblical values and that often are strokes of economic brilliance as well. That is why I refer to the seven tensions as *creative* tensions. To the seeker, business is not simply a temptation that is to be mitigated by making unprofitable economic decisions or that is to be offset by charitable activities. Rather, his business conduct becomes one more *expression* of faith.

Let's look at the example already cited between biblical warnings against a love of money and market demands to focus on making a profit. The generalist would simply duck the problem. Typically, he would respond to this dilemma with assertions about God's love, his joy in Jesus, and how the things of this world don't matter. He would also talk about how proud he is of his work and how close he'd become to his employees. The marital problems of his secretary might follow, or an extended story of his conversion, by which time the original question—about how his efforts to make a profit tie in to obedience to God's authority—would be lost.

The justifier would argue that capitalism is the best mechanism for sustaining a constitution-based society like the U.S., thereby guaranteeing freedom of religion. No problem.

Or the justifier might view a specific conflict selectively, looking only at the seemingly biblical side of the trade-offs— the obligations that are on the left side of the list of seven tensions. So he might spend X amount of effort on wealth creation of an exploitative sort (say, by cheating suppliers out of a fair profit), but it is the Y amount of effort that he spends on giving the proceeds away that captures his attention. As long as the charitable contributions are above the required tithe, his image of his own faithfulness (which is, after all, the real goal) is comfortable. Another frequent response of the justifier is to choose examples in which doing good always pays off in the end, similar to secular arguments about enlightened self-interest. He might, for example, only consider the occasions when he voluntarily disclosed a mistake to a customer and later got twice the business.

The seeker, however, would not duck, gloss over, or compartmentalize the inherent conflicts posed by modern capitalism's strong emphasis on profit and by the biblical command to submit to God's will above all else. Instead, his faith, already holistic in orientation, mediates the tension in a number of ways. It may help him gain a long-term perspective that allows him to plan and methodically balance his various obligations or help him make short-term sacrifices for the long-term health of his company, family, or own self. The seeker may draw heavily on the New Testament metaphor of the good steward, or on the Old Testament Creation mandate to increase the land, thereby setting up a quasi-agricultural view of the marketplace that allows cyclical periods of investment, harvest, and fallow seasons. This image builds a certain flexibility into his approach that rises above the make-or-break mentality of short-term survival strategies. He may instinctively or overtly base his own perception of relevant problems on New Testament injunctions to love one another, and therefore strongly favor a business approach based on concrete contributions of value and service in the marketplace rather than on something more abstract such as "the efficiencies of the markets." Because he is relationally oriented, he will generally steer clear of businesses where the deal is the only product.

In this way, profit is transformed from being an ultimate value to being *a result of ultimate values*. This is not an anticapitalistic or even an economically neutral leadership philosophy. The seeker's overt business actions and values include profit seeking and organized capital investments, but his faith mediates the process to include the "softer," more spiritual aspects of Christianity. So close are these responses to one of "enlightened self-interest" that an outsider usually cannot distinguish the difference that faith makes in the seeker's thinking.

And yet, I will maintain that the seeker's faith does indeed profoundly affect his decision making. By responding creatively, his normal tensions between business and other obligations are transformed into expressions of faith. Then a CEO's state-ment, such as "business is nothing," can coexist unhypocritically with the fact that he spends a major part of his time on business. The evangelical business leader's particular paradox, or series of paradoxes, is a creative phenomenon in that it leads to productive economic activity and to productive personal spiritual fulfillment.

In other words, for the seeker the tension between capitalistic activity and private faith is recognized and sustained instead of denied or seen as a trade-off to be dealt with in separate allotments of time and money. The crucial point here is that *the normal conflicts between the marketplace and Christian ethics are not terminally destructive for either side of the equation*. In the long run neither economics nor personal faith suffers from the other's claims, because of the way in which business is conducted and organized over time. Hence the paradoxical effect.

Where there is an undeniable contradiction between a particular business opportunity and what the seeker feels to be right in Christian terms, he either has enough slack built into the system to reject the deal or he finds a way to approach the problem that is more in line with his conscience. This kind of reframing of business problems is not accidental; it is a product of leadership and prayer.

The suggestion that the evangelical's business experiences as represented by the seeker are inherently paradoxical should not be entirely surprising, given the essentially paradoxical nature of Christianity. Many of the fundamental precepts of Christianity are themselves standing paired opposites: in death there is life; humans are essentially sinful and yet forgiven; heaven cannot be reached as a result of good deeds, and yet good deeds are evidence of faith. Such tensions are a fundamental part of the Christian identity. Life is acknowledged to have definable, inevitable limits, and yet mortality carries the element of eternal life. The evangelical is human, flawed, and sinful, and yet has an eternal soul. He or she is humbled by mortal sin and yet self-confident in being loved by God. By accepting God's love the evangelical opens the way to becoming a positive part of God's plan.

In describing the seven creative tensions, I am reminded of an early Greek pun, attributed to Heraclitus, that asserted that life was an archer's bow. The pun was based on the verbal joke that the Greek words for *bow* and *life* were the same—*bios*—only with different accentuation. The idea behind the pun was profound, because it described the world as existing in a constant state of balanced opposites—taut juxtapositions of mortality and immortality, good and evil, light and dark. Such contradictions, far from being mutually negating, were the source of creative power. Another fragment from Heraclitus also expresses this concept of the creative conflict well. He

wrote, "War is the father of all things," meaning that creative forces depend on conflict for their procreative power.

For the generalist and the justifier, conflict is almost unchristian. For the seeker, life is indeed a bow, a constant tension between the demands of the world and the promptings of the soul. Faith is the string that holds these opposing forces in balance and that makes the bow work.

The irony is that while evangelicalism can bring about a softening of the more predatory aspects of capitalistic activity and a broadening of personal definitions of success, it also nourishes an extremely powerful, focused economic and managerial expertise such as might be echoed in the most secular of business people. A good example is CEO Max De Pree, noted for his business prowess but quite different in other ways from the average tycoon. He once introduced a cap on the income gap between the highest and lowest at Herman Miller, based on a personally bothersome conversation he had had with an hourly employee. De Pree is an obvious seeker and an outstandingly innovative and successful executive.

WHAT THE SEVEN CREATIVE TENSIONS DO

The concept of the seven creative tensions provides a springboard for understanding the role of faith in the businessperson's specific worldly pursuits. Given their pervasive nature, these seven tensions outline the major building blocks of the seeker's business and career thinking. It would be an understatement to say that tracking this process is a very difficult task. It requires identifying qualitative factors and tracing their effects on concrete, materialistic actions. The seekers whose interviews are recorded here did not, for the most part, express their thoughts in neat, paradoxical statements. And yet the *totality* of their statements has suggested just such a pattern.

The following story is an excellent example of the seven creative tensions at work and of the ways that these reference points of Christian and business obligation can determine a seeker's problem solving. This story was told to me first-hand by Jack Willome, president of Rayco, a homebuilding and neighborhood development company in San Antonio, Texas.

Several years ago, our company was involved in real, life-threatening consumer litigation. The plaintiffs' attorney was very active, and he filed a group action against us. Ultimately, about one thousand families to whom we had sold homes over four or five years were included.

Here's the background. Between 1981 and 1985 we sold about thirteen thousand homes total, and approximately three thousand were sold to a company called Epic. They would hold the homes, renting them temporarily, in anticipation of the high inflation in housing prices which had been occurring in Texas. When oil collapsed, that inflation did not happen. They had made heavy acquisitions throughout the Southwest, and owned about twenty thousand homes altogether. By 1985 they were bankrupt.

Local papers reported that all of Epic's houses would be dumped at the same time, and that values in our neighborhoods would plummet.

So this attorney who advertised on TV, organized through cells with block captains in all our neighborhoods, and filed a group action lawsuit. Initially about a hundred families were involved, and the more publicity it got, the more people jumped on the bandwagon. They were motivated by fear. The truth was, none of these houses was ever dumped. The attorney was on a contingency fee, so he would only be paid on the basis of what he won for them, leaving the homeowners with no financial risk for the lawsuit.

The filing, under an anomaly in the Deceptive Trade Act of Texas, was in October '85, and our sales stayed strong till March '86. So the lawsuit was building to a crescendo just as our business was falling apart. And you have to remember that judges are elected in Texas, and this attorney was very powerful politically, and the judges were looking at two thousand homeowners. . . . So you get all the dynamics.

I wanted to lose as little money as possible for the company. I genuinely felt that the lawsuit was unfair if not downright sleazy. I wanted to be protected. I wanted to win. Those were my kind of gut desires, and that's what I asked for through prayer.

But through dialogue with some good people, I got refocused. We have this conference line, and once a month about ten of us, from all over the country, talk and pray for each other. I told the group about the lawsuit, and asked that they pray for me to win the suit.

And one of them said, "Hey, wait a minute. I can't pray for that. All I can pray for is that you be treated fairly and that the truth come out."

And, of course, he was right. And this really changed the way I looked at the case. Instead of focusing on how to win, to focus on being treated fairly and the truth coming out. So I asked my attorney some questions about the court system and our case. I asked how many of the elected judges (out of approximately eight) would give business a fair trial, and he said maybe two. So right there, it would have taken an act of God to be treated fairly, right? And the second thing he told me was that in the courtroom process attorneys use procedural rules to exclude the truth. So it would take an act of God for us to be treated

fairly and for the decision to be based on truth.

And that got down to something I could pray for with integrity and I could ask other people to pray for with integrity.

During a forty-five-day period I sat through the depositions. I wanted to hear firsthand what people were saying they'd gone through and understand what this case was really about. It was very painful for me, but it gave me a perspective that I couldn't have gotten just talking to our attorneys. You know, you just naturally tend to exaggerate your own position.

Ultimately, I came to the conclusion that the more I knew about both sides, the better equipped I was to . . . well, it just hit me that it was foolishness to put the fate of our company in the hands of the jury and a judge in this crazy process. What I needed to do was to inject myself directly into negotiations and apply what I saw of the truth, instead of getting ourselves into this radical position we tend to get into— that I tend to get myself into—of black and white, wrong and right, good and bad. . . . The world just isn't that way.

Ultimately we settled the case. And those prayers were answered over and over again.

That's one of the things I've learned from all this. When I look at things from the standpoint of good and bad, right and wrong, I end up projecting my own garbage on other people. When I look for the guilt in others, I usually see my own guilt. When I look for the innocence, I'll usually find my own innocence. And I believe that where the compassion of Christ comes in is to be able to see the innocence of people who are attacking us.

Jack's account is a moving example of the power of prayer in a CEO's decision making. Moreover, we can see in his story all seven of the tensions that are identified in this book. Let's look at how each of these tensions became a creative force after Jack's views were changed through prayer.

Jack did not ignore the money side of this problem, and yet he created a new solution that he saw as being consistent with and motivated by his faith *(Tension 1—the love for God and the pursuit of profit)*. He was acutely aware that the stakes were high and that the company was on the line. At first, he simply wanted to win, in order to prevent the loss of revenue that an adverse judgment would impose. As he revised his view of the problem, however, he began to see the issue as one of both poor stewardship and unchristian self-centeredness in adopting a winner-take-all strategy *(Tension 2—love and the competitive drive)*. He did not adopt an *uncompetitive* strategy, because he was always acutely aware that the

financial life of the company was at stake. He did, however, radically revise the terms of *winning* and his subsequent negotiating strategy as a result of his changed views.

Note that Jack did not arrive at this strategy through reasoned self-interest (for example, *it simply pays to settle out of court),* but through a sense of love and fairness—a love of God and a love of the people testifying against the firm. As a good steward, as a person striving to serve God, as a Christian commanded to love his neighbor and directed by biblical injunctions not to lie, Jack voluntarily submitted himself to the humbling experience of hearing his company's actions described in the worst, most distorted terms. We can appreciate how difficult it would be for anyone, but especially for the head of a company, to do this face to face. Can you imagine former Ford Motor chairman Lee Iacocca appearing in person at the Ford Pinto depositions?

At the same time, it would be wrong to characterize Jack's actions, though requiring humility, as being passive. Resisting the temptation to win at any cost in order to protect his personal image of "success" required tremendous leadership and self-confidence *(Tension 4—humility and the ego of success)*. Negotiating a settlement that would not bankrupt the company demanded strong leadership ability.

Jack's decision to attend the depositions and to seek the truth by listening to people made him sensitive to the double-sided nature of the problem *(Tension 3—people needs and profit obligations)*. Whereas earlier he had seen the people in his neighborhoods as being in total and illegitimate opposition to the profit needs of his company, he realized after hearing them that, however unfair the lawsuit, they had a case and a need, too.

Later on, Jack's new sensitivity was put to economic advantage. The settlements were never contested. Afterward Jack's organization initiated a new market study of people's expectations in the starter housing market. They discovered a number of surprising preferences in new home owners that led to a very different design and construction strategy. In the late 1980s his firm was able to create a forty-five thousand-dollar start-up house in southern Texas, and was the first real estate company in his region to experience an upturn in its market, well ahead of other competitors in the area. This combination of charity toward his adversaries and the later creation of a successful new product puts *Tension 6—charity and wealth* into a creative combination rather than into the position of paired opposites concerning the giving and getting of money. What of *Tension 5—family and work?* Jack himself referred to this aspect of his life when he summarized the experience. He reported that his family had been extremely supportive during these events, and that they had given him

the strength to endure the stress of the depositions and settlements. He said that they became increasingly close as he went through the trial. This, too, underscored the element of love and truth in the process. As he put it, "The closer I get to them, the more I can tell my family where I *really* am." For Jack—a recovering alcoholic, who had once been isolated and without intimate relationships—this was an extraordinary admission.

Relationships played a significant role also in Jack's attention to this devotional life. Like many evangelicals, he has formed networks of friends (many of them other CEOs) who support each other and pray for each other. As we can see from this incident, these groups are restrictive in a social sense; but they also played a mediating function between the demands of outsiders and the demands of Christian faith *(Tension 7—faithful witness in the secular city)*. They helped Jack to *survive* in the real world rather than to withdraw from it.

So it is possible to see how evangelicalism as described earlier (prayerful, personal, relational, and intensifying) became a mediating, transformational factor in each of the tensions inherent in Jack's situation. Jack himself experienced several important inner transformations as a result of his fellowship with the prayer group and their subsequent prayers for him. He went from a win-lose, self-regarding, seemingly hopeless situation to one of truth seeking and, ultimately, accommodation. Also—and this is very much to the point of this study—he developed an economically viable strategy to deal with the crisis.

It's apparent that Jack's faith is what transformed his personal experience of a business crisis into a more humanizing experience, consistent with Christian ethics. His faith was also a catalyst for wealth creation.

Jack's story is a particularly organized display of the seven creative tensions at work. In many other interviews, I had to piece together the creative aspect of the tensions over more than one event to capture the full impact of faith in these leaders' thinking. For this reason, it is important to understand that this study is an analysis of the *process* of evangelical business leadership rather than the *ethics* of individual acts. It is not just an ordering of the facts of a CEO's decision making, but rather an ordering of his construction of reality.

The seven categories, or creative tensions, suggested here give us an organizing framework for understanding how some of the most admired evangelical business leaders in America deal with the profound tensions of modern life and especially of human economic experience. This framework helps us understand also the nature of a certain type of business leadership which addresses key choices that Christians in business face.

Interestingly, when this story and the seven tensions were presented to a group of evangelical CEOs, one of them, who was president of a major fast food chain, found his own thinking changing dramatically about a serious business problem he was facing. He, too, was being sued in a particularly vicious class action case which had been publicized nationwide, accusing him among other things of being ethnically prejudiced. For his part, he felt he was simply carrying out the letter of a contract. After hearing Jack's struggle, this other CEO, call him Tom, changed both the way he himself thought about his legal "enemy" and the way the case was being handled. Against the advice of his lawyers, he met with the man personally and discovered that serious problems of communication had occurred on both sides. They eventually made a settlement. They even became friends.

When Tom's son expressed amazement that his father was going to meet with the man who had publicly portrayed him in such a negative way, Tom told his son of his own spiritual trials over this case, and his change of thinking. Tom reported that he and his son had never had such a frank talk about religion, and in the end he flew his son to one of the meetings to meet "the enemy."

Stories such as these are not just about the ethics of business or profitable financial outcomes. They show how the evangelical CEO's faith can help him sustain and creatively manage the opposing demands upon him through changing something very deep inside himself, namely his attitudes, his sense of others, his willingness to take risks.

I see the framework offered here as useful even to nonevangelicals who would seek a more domesticated, humanized version of advanced capitalism. Consider the comment of a very successful, extremely driven nonevangelical executive in the financial services world. He was describing the philosophy of his firm and his own managerial style: Motivate people on greed, and as long as you can control the greed to stay within legal bounds, you have an unstoppable economic machine. The only problem, he mused, was that people burned out. The system exploited their strength, then spat them out with nothing left but their bank accounts (if they were lucky). He himself said he felt very fortunate "to have a wife who is willing to spend all her time raising my kids. Because I never see them."

I asked him how long he could keep up the pace. He admitted that, because he was forty-one years old, he had only a few years left. The worry, however, was in deciding what to do next. He couldn't just quit, as a friend of his had done, to farm land in Australia.

The problem is that I don't want to stop working, and I can't keep up this game forever. But I don't know how to do it any other way. What I need is some sort of mental halfway house.

For the evangelical business leaders of the seeker category—who also are prone to "doing something economic" but are subject to the tensions between hard work, ambition, and the "softer" aspects of existence—Christian faith is that mental halfway house.

PART THREE
The Tools

from the editors of *The Life@Work Journal*

. . .

Larry Burkett is quick to point out that he wasn't the first person to use the Bible as a study guide for operating a business. In fact, Burkett notes in *Business by the Book* that there was a time in American history when most universities were "biblical schools training future business leaders." In other words, Scripture was foundational for *everyone* who was training for a leadership role in the marketplace.

If culture hadn't changed so dramatically, Burkett could have spent his time doing something more constructive than penning a how-to manual on running a Biblically based business. But by 1990, when Burkett's book came out, the influencers of society—the media, the academic world, etc.—had driven a wedge between faith and work.

Burkett, whose expertise is in financial management, considered his book "a radical approach to business management," and to this day no other book so thoroughly lines out practical ways to set up and run a business according to God's Word. Much of his advice flies in the face of conventional wisdom, but it challenges us to pursue and trust God in the day-to-day reality of business.

In this chapter, Burkett outlines his six "minimums" for doing business by the Book—reflecting Christ in our business practices, being accountable, providing a quality product at a fair price, honoring our creditors, treating our employees fairly and treating our customers fairly.

Such tactics aren't always profitable in a worldly sense. In fact, Burkett tells us up front that it will cost us money. Neither are they always easy to implement.

"I myself find that applying these minimums is a continual challenge," he writes. "They are particularly difficult to follow when those we encounter in business—even our own coworkers—rarely attempt to do the same."

In defining these minimums and the struggle to meet them, Burkett supports the idea that although Scripture establishes the criterion upon which to build a successful work life, a significant tension regularly exists between what God wants and what the professional environment demands. How one reconciles such tensions is an earmark of integrity.

Burkett recognizes what previous generations understood so well—there's an eternal payoff to doing business by the Book.

7 Basic Biblical Minimums

from *Business by the Book* by Larry Burkett

WHENEVER MOST PEOPLE think about the basic minimums of Christianity, they generally think of the Ten Commandments. Indeed, these are the minimums that God said would separate His people from those around them. In the business environment, the same commandments obviously apply, but there are some other minimums that set apart God's followers from others in the business world.

These are not lofty, obscure goals for us to fantasize about, but rather outside indicators of whether we are serious about dedicating our business to the Lord. I myself find that applying these minimums is a continual challenge. They are particularly difficult to follow when those we encounter in business—even our own coworkers—rarely attempt to do the same. Yet God's best is to do unto others as we would *desire* they do unto us, not to do unto others as they *do* unto us.

REFLECT CHRIST IN YOUR BUSINESS PRACTICES

Let me say up front that I have no doubt that if you determine to adopt this one principle in your business it will cost you money. We live in a society that thrives on deception and tricky contracts. Anyone operating in a manner that glorifies Christ will be faced with many opportunities to suffer.

Take for example the practice of total honesty. Proverbs 3:32 says, "For the crooked man is an abomination to the Lord; / But He is intimate with the upright." And Proverbs 4:24 says, "Put away from you a deceitful mouth, / And put devious lips far from you." Both of these verses imply the same basic principle: Honesty is rewarded and dishonesty punished. If the issue were just to steal or not steal, most of God's people would have no problem in obeying. But in real-life situations that principle gets a little sticky.

Paul was a retired business executive who moved to Mexico to operate a large cattle ranch. His business was prospering because he chose to pay his Mexican employees well and operated his ranch in a manner that was pleasing to the Lord. His only real problem was in buying equipment in the United States and then having it shipped into Mexico. He quickly learned that if he didn't bribe the border guards and several local officials along the way, his equipment might never make it to his ranch.

Paul knew that bribes were illegal in Mexico. But he also knew they were a way of life and an accepted business practice—outside of official channels, of course.

During a visit to the U.S., Paul attended a Business by the Book seminar in Texas. He felt convinced that this one area of his business did not honor the Lord and made a decision not to bribe anyone to transport the equipment he had just purchased. As expected the equipment was stopped at the first border station because of "irregularities." After many attempts to get the equipment released, Paul asked the local customs official, "What would it take to have the paperwork corrected?"

He was told that the delay could be eliminated for a "fee" of two hundred American dollars—a small price to pay when compared to the value of the equipment.

Paul had already decided that he would not pay a bribe, no matter what the price, so he refused the offer. As a result he had to go on to his ranch without his equipment. Several days later, the equipment still had not arrived, so Paul began to make some inquiries. After considerable effort he found out that his equipment had been stripped and many of the parts sold on the black market. What he ulti-

mately recovered represented only a fraction of the original value.

Because of this event Paul decided to sell the ranch, move back to the U.S., and reestablish his operation. The move cost him several thousand dollars and the loss of some more equipment when crossing back into our country, but he felt he had virtually no other choice based on his conviction not to pay bribes.

Incidentally, this story did have a happy ending. A few months after Paul moved, he learned that the Mexican government had appropriated many of the ranches owned by foreigners in the very district where he had been operating. Had he stayed any longer, he would likely have received only a fraction of his ranch's value.

BE ACCOUNTABLE

Perhaps nothing in our society is more needed for those in positions of authority than accountability. Too often those with authority are able (and willing) to surround themselves with people who support their decisions without question. This may seem like an asset initially, but in the long run it becomes a liability. Why? Because without a system of checks and balances, anyone will eventually drift off course. If you don't believe this, just try to find an example of anyone who operated without accountability and stayed on his or her original course.

Even David, the king that God Himself

chose, drifted off course when he listened to his generals, who told him he was too valuable to be risking his life in battle. Completely forgetting that God had brought him through many battles without difficulty, David believed their accolades. (Accolades become easy to believe when you want to hear them!) He stayed in town while his army fought. The result? That infamous episode with Bathsheba, which ultimately created strife within his household.

Many businesspeople think they are accountable because they operate with a board of directors or hold regular staff meetings. I have attended enough board meetings to know that most boards under the direction of a strong leader are simply rubber stamps. And only a rare staff member will confront the boss's directives once he or she has laid out a course, even if that course is in total contrast to the original goals and objectives of the company.

So what is the answer? I believe God's Word offers several. One is to seek the counsel of your spouse. This is important for any married person in a leadership position. Since more men run businesses than women I'll direct my comments to them, but the principles apply equally to women in business. Most husbands virtually ignore the counsel of their wives when it comes to making business decisions. And yet God's Word clearly says that he made husband and wife to

become one person: "For this cause a man shall leave his father and his mother, and shall cleave to his wife; and they shall become one flesh" (Gen. 2:24). Is this relationship limited to a nonbusiness relationship only? If so, then find the reference in God's Word!

A valid argument can be made that often the wife doesn't know anything about the business. The solution is to start sharing the major decisions so that she *will* know something when the need arises. All too often the wife doesn't *want* to know anything about the business. I would answer, "That isn't an option according to God's Word. When a wife takes on the responsibilities of a helpmate, then she must be willing to learn enough to help."

I have been continually amazed at some of the insights wives bring to a discussion of subjects they supposedly know little or nothing about. For example, a few years ago I was counseling with a Christian fabric manufacturer who was in a real quandary about selling his business. The whole industry was facing severe competition from the Chinese, and it appeared certain that many of the major manufacturers would move their operations to Taiwan to reduce their overhead. This man's wife, who had been meeting with us at my insistence, stated during one meeting that she didn't think he should sell.

"Why not?" he snapped, his body language clearly indicating that he didn't value her opinion in business matters very highly. At first she retreated back into her submissive-wife role and didn't say anything further.

"Come on, Jackie," I urged, "if you have something to add, don't be bullied into silence. That's not meek; it's weak." The husband sat in glaring silence as he refused to meet my eyes.

"Well, I just believe that God gave us this business in an industry heavily dominated by Jewish people," she said, glancing cautiously in her husband's direction. "If we don't stick it out, probably nobody will. If we have built a firm foundation, I believe we should be able to compete with the Chinese. Maybe we can find a product that they can't make as well as we can."

"What do you mean?" I asked, watching as a shocked look spread across her husband's face.

"I believe we should concentrate on developing our own line of denims," she suggested, really getting enthusiastic now. "I've noticed that the communist countries are importing larger quantities of blue jeans and other such products. Why couldn't we get the government to sponsor our export of these products, like they sponsor food products?"

I told her the idea had a lot of merit if the details could be worked out.

Her husband also perked up a little and said he had had a similar idea but had never explored it. Then his countenance fell again.

"What's wrong?" I asked.

"We don't have the capital to make the changeover or to survive until a good product can be found," he replied dejectedly. "And no banker is going to advance the money for such a speculative idea."

"What do you think, Jackie?" I asked.

"I believe we could start an employees' cooperative and sell them an interest in the company," Jackie said excitedly. "After all, it's their jobs that are on the line. We could sell out the company and the brand names we own and live comfortably for the rest of our lives, but they will be forced out into a declining labor market."

"You know, that's a possibility I hadn't considered before," Jackie's husband mused. "It's just possible that the employees might be willing to put up the money in return for a piece of the company. But if we do it and it fails, we will have severely diluted our ownership."

"We started with nothing twenty years ago," Jackie responded gently. "I guess we could start the same way again if we had to. Besides, I'd rather try and fail than to fold our tents and fade away. There just aren't enough companies seeking to serve Christ in the garment industry; we can't afford to let this one go."

"Where in the world did you learn about the fabric business?" the husband asked. "And where did you hear about employee buyouts?"

Jackie replied, with just the slightest trace of a smile on her face, "You forget I was your only help when we began. And just because I stayed home to raise our children, it doesn't mean I let my brain atrophy."

Jackie and her husband did sell nearly half of the business to their employees and developed a thriving export business to the Communist East-bloc countries. They have since retired, and now they spend several months each year setting up jointly owned dealerships with Christians from the communist countries. This latest venture has been a tool for reaching a previously unreachable group of people.

SET UP AN ACCOUNTABILITY GROUP

A businessperson can also set up an impartial group of Christian advisers. I know that in many areas of the country finding qualified Christians who will agree to serve in this capacity may be difficult. An alternative is to link up with one or two others in similar businesses in other parts of the country and communicate on major decisions by phone or other means.

I have participated in such groups, and even now my advisers and I meet by telephone at least once every couple of months, or as a specific need arises. I have found that my willingness to ask their counsel and advice makes them more likely to do the same with others.

Our accountability group has even helped resolve business disputes. For instance, two Christian businessmen entered an informal partnership to purchase some real estate. They agreed that one partner, Ralph, would put up the funds and the other, Gene, would develop and manage the property. As time passed, however, Ralph discovered that large transfers of funds had been made from his corporate account, and little or no money had been returned. When he asked his partner for an accounting, Gene became quite offended and refused to discuss the issue at all.

Ralph then *demanded* an accounting under the threat of legal action, to which Gene responded, "Go ahead! I know I haven't done anything wrong. I sent all your money back."

Because Ralph didn't want to sue a brother, he asked for my help in resolving the matter. I just happened to be part of an accountability group with Gene, so I felt I could discuss the subject directly with him. But I quickly found that Gene was also highly offended by my being involved; he hung up in the middle of our conversation. Later he called to apologize and to explain his side of the issue.

"I feel as if I am doing Ralph a favor by managing the properties without a fee, and I resent being accused of diverting funds," Gene told me. "All the funds have been wired directly into our company account, and if Ralph had just checked the wire transfers, he would have known everything was okay."

Two opposing issues were at work in this highly informal partnership. First, Gene, the managing partner, had operated as an individual entrepreneur for so long that he had a difficult time when anyone doubted his judgment or motives. Second, Ralph, the capital partner, ran a company that wired thousands of money transfers each month, making it highly probable that money wired into his company could be misallocated if it was not identified properly.

An analysis of the wire transfers to Ralph's company showed the money had indeed been returned (with a profit). The friendship was salvaged, even though the partnership was dissolved. But without the open forum of an accountability group it is quite possible that a lawsuit would have been instituted and a permanent rift created. Everyone needs accountability, especially those who don't have to accept it!

PROVIDE A QUALITY PRODUCT AT A FAIR PRICE

The value of the products and services a company offers says more to the public about the real character of the company and its people than perhaps any other aspect of the company's life. Value can be defined as the effective return on a purchase. Low initial cost does not necessarily represent value. But when a Christian business accepts the standard for service

and products that the Bible prescribes, the end result will be the best product at the best possible price.

I once read an article about a doctor who stopped charging fees and went to a "set your own fee" policy. When a patient came in for a visit, the receptionist would give the person information on the payment policy, as well as a detailed analysis of the costs of office overhead and insurance. Then the patient was asked to pay what he or she thought was fair.

To be sure, some patients paid poorly because they thought this doctor was a sucker. But the doctor's overall income increased by approximately ten percent after he switched from the fixed fee structure. Apparently his patients felt they were receiving value for his services.

Another great example of this principle is Chic-Fil-A, Inc., headquartered in Atlanta. This company's Christian leadership takes pride in the quality of their products. They spend little or no money on national advertising, and yet they are one of the three fastest growing fast food chains in the United States.

Chic-Fil-A closes its stores on Sunday, in contrast to the other fast food businesses located in the same shopping malls, and they pay their employees well (even providing college scholarships). So how do they survive and even contrive to grow? Chic-Fil-A simply gives away free samples of its food in the mall when the company opens a new store. The management knows that once chicken lovers taste the product, they will return with their friends. The best advertisement any company can have is a satisfied customer.

The norm in our society today seems to be: Deliver the least product possible at the highest price. But this works only during good times, when little or no competition exists.

For Christians to follow the philosophy of providing high quality at fair prices says a lot about their spiritual commitment. When you truly love others more than yourself, you want them to get the best deal possible. In the process, you will also prosper.

HONOR YOUR CREDITORS

Business creditors include those who have loaned you merchandise as well as those who have loaned you money. Too often in our modern business environment, suppliers are treated like a no-interest source of operating capital. When business is slow, it is considered normal to delay paying suppliers to offset the reduced cash flow.

Now, if the situation is beyond your control, that's one thing. But if you are simply choosing a cheaper way to operate, you are violating a biblical principle. Proverbs 3:27-28 suggests,

> Do not withhold good from those to
> whom it is due.

> When it is in your power to do it.
> Do not say to your neighbor, "Go, and
>   come back,
> And tomorrow I will give it,"
> When you have it with you.

A Christian who continues to order materials and other supplies when there are already past-due bills is being deceitful. That may be hard for you to hear, but just place yourself in the supplier's position. Would you want someone ordering your materials under an implied promise to pay when he or she already has demonstrated that the business was losing money? Or would you want a customer to delay paying you, rather than borrowing the money at interest to pay for the materials?

I was teaching a seminar to a group of businesspeople, and I mentioned in passing that to delay paying suppliers because customers were slow in paying their bills was wrong. One of the participants stopped me and said, "Do you mean that if I don't pay my bills because I'm not getting paid it's a sin?"

"No, that is not what I mean," I replied. "It's only a sin if you know it's wrong and still persist in doing it."

"But what if paying all my bills would cause me to lose the business?" he asked in a somewhat defiant tone.

I used the standard response I always use in similar situations: "Are we discussing a real situation or a hypothetical one?"

"What do you mean?" he asked as he began to get the drift of my question.

"Well, if paying your suppliers would really cost you your business when it might otherwise survive, I would suggest contacting the suppliers and allowing them to have a part in the decision. I'm sure most of them would be willing to work with you, rather than see the business fail."

"Well, it wouldn't really cause my business to fail," he admitted reluctantly, then added, "but it might in someone's else business."

"True," I agreed, "and if that's the case, then that person would need to face that issue at that time. God doesn't hold us responsible for what we can't do, only for what we can. But if the decision is purely economic—in other words, it's simply cheaper to finance the cash flow by owing a supplier than owing the bank, then it's wrong."

The same seminar participant later said, "You have convinced me that I should borrow the funds and pay my suppliers what is due. My company can easily absorb the interest payments. I just delayed payment because my accountant encouraged me to 'stiff' the suppliers."

Integrity is a rare commodity in our generation, especially where other people's money is concerned. A Christian who wants to have a credible witness needs to meet at least this minimum standard. I recall a note I received in 1976 from the chairman of one of the largest paper companies in America. It simply said, "Thank you for the integrity you have shown in paying your bills to our company."

I thought that was remarkable because our total purchases for the previous year couldn't have been ten thousand dollars—certainly only a fraction of their total sales. So I decided to call the chairman to ask why he wrote the note.

He said, "Your ministry is one of the few Christian organizations we deal with that pays its bills on time—every time. I'm a Christian also, but the delinquencies among churches and other ministries has become a source of ridicule in some of our directors' meetings."

It is remarkable that the head of a major company would be subjected to ridicule from his peers for the failure of Christian-run organizations to pay their bills on time. Small wonder that many people avoid doing business with Christians!

TREAT YOUR EMPLOYEES FAIRLY

Fairness is both a responsibility and an opportunity. The employer who practices fairness is able to share Christ with his or her employees because he "practices what he preaches," as the old saying goes. To be sure, some employees will take offense against a manager or employer no matter what that person does. But that's their problem. Those in positions of authority need to be concerned only with their own actions.

Fairness is usually related to issues of pay and benefits in the work environment, but that is not the total picture. Fairness also involves attitudes and relationships. For example, if the tendency is for managers to look down (socially or intellectually) on lower-strata workers, that attitude will be transmitted and received. Once the employees recognize that a social barrier has been erected, any effort to evangelize will usually be rejected.

The first step in establishing the principle of fairness is to recognize that all people are important, regardless of their vocational position. I first recognized this principle while in the Air Force. The barriers between the enlisted and commissioned personnel were real and absolute. The armed services deliberately create this separation in an attempt to make the ruling group (officers) seem infallible. They perceive this as a necessary ingredient in issuing life-and-death orders.

Unfortunately, that same mentality has been carried over into business relationships. Perhaps this is a reflection of the master-slave mentality, even though we abandoned the actual practice of slavery more than one hundred years ago. But Jesus did not establish any such artificial barriers between Himself and His disciples, nor did He ever allow them to do so between themselves and the people they desired to reach.

If you find that you can't give the same honor and regard to the lowest-ranked employee in your business, you need to stop right here and resolve this issue with the Lord. The second chapter of James covers this issue thoroughly, summing it up in verse 9: "But if you show partiality, you are committing sin and are convicted by the law as transgressors."

I saw a practical application of this principle as a young Christian. Our pastor was being reviewed for a salary increase. The chairman of the board of deacons presented to the entire church its recommendation of an increase of several thousand dollars a year, and the church body unanimously approved the increase. Then the chairman presented the recommendation for the custodian's salary, which was several thousand dollars a year less than the pastor's.

The pastor stopped the meeting and asked, "Why are we willing to pay me more than the janitor when he has more children and fewer benefits?"

The chairman was taken back by the question. The reason was obvious, although unspoken: you don't pay janitors what you pay senior pastors. That's called "the Indian-chief principle." The chairman replied, "Pastor, we can't afford that much of a pay increase."

"Then give him part of my increase," the pastor commented. "I really don't need more money, and I'm sure he does."

The meeting ended that evening without

any resolution. Eventually, however, the deacon board did recommend giving the custodian a substantial raise (almost to the pastor's salary). And the events of that evening had a profound effect on the attitudes of the entire congregation. I was certainly challenged to examine everything I do on the basis of God's Word, not what is normal practice.

TREAT YOUR CUSTOMERS FAIRLY

If you truly believe that your greatest responsibility is to be a faithful witness for the Lord, then your greatest outreach will be with those closest to you. In your business, this applies to your creditors, who will listen because you pay your bills on time and treat them fairly. It applies to your employees, who will listen because you treat them with honor and pay them fairly. And it certainly applies to your customers, who will take you seriously because you give them a good product at a fair price and stand behind your word.

I saw this principle applied in a practical way in my own life several years ago when I was in the electronics business. I was calling on a potential customer for one of our products, a computerized circuit tester. This particular product was fairly expensive, about twenty-five thousand dollars, but performed a function that would save a qualified user several times that amount each year. However, this potential customer didn't seem to

have a need for a twenty-five-thousand-dollar circuit tester. He appeared to be a test equipment "buff" who wanted to own every new piece of test equipment made. He had already talked himself into buying the product even before I was finished explaining it. Without a doubt our tester would have helped his operation, but he would not have been able to recover its cost in his application.

We needed the sale at the time, and he was totally committed to buying. But even as I took the contract papers out of my briefcase, I could hear the words of the apostle Paul ringing in my ears: "Do nothing from selfishness or empty conceit, but with humility of mind let each of you regard one another as more important than himself" (Phil. 2:3). I stopped and said, "I can't sell this equipment to you."

"Why not?" he asked with some indignation. "I can afford it. Do you need some money up front?"

"No," I replied, "the money is not the problem. It's just that I know you won't be able to recover the cost of the equipment with your volume of work. I think you would regret it later, and I'd feel like I had dumped our equipment on you."

His expression changed from indignation to surprise. Then he smiled. He then told me he appreciated my willingness to lose the sale, but he had already assessed the same issue. He planned to use the equipment to start a new line of business—repairing equipment for other small companies similar to his. I readily agreed that the equipment would be perfectly suited for that function, and we closed the deal.

I had several opportunities to meet with that man over the next few years, and we became good friends. The death of his youngest child eventually caused him to seek my counsel, and I had the privilege of leading him to the Lord. I truly believe the process began when I felt the conviction to put his needs first and treat him fairly.

Now, twenty years later, the twenty-five thousand dollars he paid our company has long since been spent, and the equipment I sold him has long since worn out. The one thing that still survives is our mutual love for the Lord. That sale will last for an eternity.

from the editors of *The Life@Work Journal*

. . .

As the senior vice president of a college, William Pollard knew all about the value of education. But he really went to school when he interviewed for an executive position with ServiceMaster.

Pollard measured the corporate landscape with his considerable expertise and realized that if he joined the company he immediately would be in line for the CEO's job. What, he asked during the interview, would he need to do to eventually make that jump?

It was at that point that the interview ended and the lesson began.

"If you want to come to ServiceMaster and contribute," Pollard later was told, "you have a wonderful opportunity. If you are coming for a particular position or title or the recognition, then just forget it."

Pollard joined the company and, in time, he became its CEO. Under his leadership, ServiceMaster has grown and shareholders have profited, while remaining true to the Biblical principles upon which it originally was founded. Pollard outlines these principles in *The Soul of the Firm*, which was published in 1996. One of those principles, as you might expect from one of the world's top service organizations, is serving others. Another is a commitment to lifelong learning—not just for the leadership team, but for the entire organization.

This chapter from *The Soul of the Firm* establishes the importance of continuing education and demonstrates how it is accomplished at ServiceMaster. "The modern-day firm," Pollard writes, "must be a learning organization. Learning and innovation go hand in hand."

ServiceMaster uses a five-step teaching process that it calls JST (job skill training) to help pass along basic skills, but the philosophy is more than task-oriented. Lifelong learners always are in pursuit of eternal truths, and the recognition that there is an ultimate source of truth is a driving force behind ServiceMaster's approach. Because God's transcendent truth is part of the equation, there is room not only for training that relates to specifics, but also for training that relates to values.

Pollard's experience supports the lessons learned at work principle, which suggests that opportunity, disciplines and pressure in the marketplace play a primary role in our continuous learning, growth, and maturity in Christ.

ServiceMaster's commitment to improving its workers was part of the vision Pollard saw when he first was recruited to the company. As founder Marion E. Wade once put it, "The pursuit of excellence is what broadens people and their horizons. This is the pursuit of excellence that the Lord requires of us, as a company and as individuals, and in such a company each individual feels that he is not merely a cog in a machine, but a cog without which the machine can't run."

8

Learning Is Everybody's Business

from *The Soul of the Firm* by William Pollard

SEVERAL YEARS AGO the ServiceMaster board of directors had a two-day session with Peter Drucker. The purpose of our time was to review how we could be more effective in our planning and governance. Peter started off the seminar with one of his famous questions: "What is your business?" The responses were varied and included the identification of markets we serve, such as our health care, education, and residential; and the services we deliver, such as food service, housekeeping, and maid service.

After about five minutes of listening to the responses regarding our markets and services, Peter told our board something that I have never been able to tell them. He said, "You are all wrong. Your business is simply the training and development of people. You package it all different ways to meet the needs and demands of the customer, but your basic business is people training and motivation. You are delivering services. You can't deliver services without people. You can't deliver quality service to the customer without motivated and trained people."

In a few short sentences, Peter brought home the point we needed to hear. Learning is basic to what we are all about as a service company. And even if your company is not in the service industry, I contend that the opportunity to learn is the best thing you can give to your workers.

But you may ask, "What is the purpose of the firm—to educate or to produce profits? Is the employee a worker or a student? Do we install systems to control and regulate people to act like robots and produce uniform results, or do we look at the variance in performance or even the mistake as an opportunity to learn?"

The modern-day firm must be a learning organization. Learning and innovation go hand in hand. The arrogance of success is to think that what you did yesterday will be sufficient for tomorrow. Leaders must set the pace as both teachers and learners.

The problem for most of us is that we define education by a diploma or a degree or lack thereof. But in reality learning is a lifelong experience. It cannot be limited to a particular teacher, school, or time in our lives. We will never achieve or learn so much that we can rest at the level of our present understanding. We have a lifetime to learn, and it is in our work environment where most of this learning can take place. Learning should be the business of the firm, and the opportunities provided should expand beyond areas directly related to the business.

I never made it as an accountant, and those in the accounting area of our business often have to put up with some of my "different" accounting ideas or questions. But my good friend Ernie Mrozek, our chief financial officer, never seems to grow weary of teaching me, and in the process, we have both learned some new ways to account for a service business. At times I have been frustrated as I have sought to understand the rationale behind certain accounting rules. But I have learned from Ernie as he has consistently applied an even hand in his teaching and management of me and the rules. He has led me as he has served and taught.

Education within the firm is not the function of any one department. If a manager is too busy to teach, he is too busy to work for ServiceMaster. Teaching enhances the process of understanding. To encourage teaching, we must openly reward those who mentor and develop others. As we look for those people who are ready for promotion, we take into account their enthusiasm for teaching. Which of their subordinates have they helped to develop?

At the same time, we must be careful not to transfer the responsibility of learning from the student to the teacher. The student is not the work product. He is the worker. The student's active participation and ownership in the results is essential.

This principle is evident even in the teaching methods we use for basic job skill training. JST, as we call it, is primarily used to teach task-oriented work, or "doing rather than being." The process is performed one on one to eliminate the group dynamic of the fear of asking "dumb" questions.

The five-step teaching process starts with a supervisor or team leader explaining the task, then performing the task while explaining it further. The leader then asks the student to perform the task while the leader provides coaching. When this step has been mastered, the student must in turn teach the task to the leader and be prepared to teach it to another student. It is in this step that learning is accelerated. And finally, the teacher and the student learn together how to inspect the work, which closes the loop.

WHY DO WE LEARN?

Learning is not just another avenue of self enrichment. The ultimate measure of learning should include a reproductive cycle. The student becomes a teacher and then becomes involved in the process of passing it on. This type of learning results in changed behavior that benefits others.

We live in a world of change. Change often stimulates learning and provides the opportunity for people to adapt and learn. Max De Pree has used the phrase "the gift of change." But people often fear change. They do not accept it as a gift. In this crucible of uncertainty, there is opportunity for positive direction, provided that those of us who lead are also ready to learn in the changing process. Change in a learning environment provides the leader with a strategic intercept point to interject the new; and cause those in the firm to rethink their assumptions and better understand each other and their relationships with others. Without change there is no innovation, creativity, or incentive for improvement. Those who initiate change will have a better opportunity to manage the change that is inevitable.

A FIRM OR A UNIVERSITY?

My vision of learning as it relates to the firm goes beyond training for a specific task or project. Executives who seek comfort in the experience of past successes and do not flood their lives with reading, listening, teaching, testing, and new experiences are soon arrogant in their own ignorances and are not leading the firm as a learning environment. A long pattern of success often breeds complacency, which undermines vitality and competitiveness of the firm. Accelerated change and diversity of thought and behavior require flexibility and adaptability within a framework of a continuum of learning. To maintain focus and direction, the leader must not only state and live the beliefs and mission of the firm, but must also allow for the testing of such beliefs and mission. She must maintain a competency and relevancy so that she can be an advocate and provide an apologetic for the belief. The firm, then, is like a university, and continuous learning is an integral part of its vitality. Thomas Jefferson's words for the University of Virginia ring true for a firm with a soul: "For here we are not afraid to follow truth wherever it may lead, or to tolerate error so long as reason is left free to combat it."

Too often the education process orients a student to please the teacher by giving the "right" answers and avoiding mistakes. I can recall several students I knew who learned to "play back" the information they were given just so they could pass a test. But did they really learn anything? This happens frequently in the work environment as well. Awards are often geared toward performing for someone else's approval rather than working to improve the product of the firm or service to the customer. As a firm grows as a learning environment, we must avoid the cycle of just pleasing the boss, and continue to test for understanding and a corresponding result in changed behavior. As this occurs, the teacher and the learner see the value of their efforts as they provide a benefit to others. When people are working for a cause that can be understood within the context of a mission, the firm and the university become one.

THE SEARCH FOR TRUTH

I believe that learning should spring from a quest for truth. We have found that people can learn to accept and apply value systems as they relate to others in their environment. In so doing, they can learn about who they are; where they came from, and who they may or may not become. In the process, I believe we should recognize and confront a basic issue of life: Is there an ultimate source of truth? Is there room for God?

Allan Bloom, in his book *The Closing of the American Mind,* concluded that the average student attending a college or university today has determined that everything is relative and there is no truth. In such an environment, there is no longer a search for truth. In the absence of searching, there can be no real learning, and therefore we are witnessing the gradual closing of the American mind. The acceptance that there can be truth and the continued process of searching for how truth can be understood and applied are at the heart of our training and development program at ServiceMaster.

This is a living principle that allows us to confront life's difficulties and failures with the reassurance that our starting point never changes and provides a reason and hope above it all. It provides a standard of integrity as we teach and learn with a potential to improve what we do and to enhance who we are becoming.

Several years ago I participated in a class with students from the Harvard Business School. As they were reviewing a case study on ServiceMaster, one of the students asked me a question about our first objective. She said, "Mr. Pollard, in a diverse and pluralistic world with people holding many different types of beliefs, your first objective—'To honor God in all we do'— must offend some people. Couldn't you get the same thing done and just eliminate that first objective?"

You know my answer to that question. But at Harvard you just can't say "no"; you have to give a reason. My response to the student was that, if our first objective had no other purpose than for her to ask the question, then it should be there. The issue of whether there is a God is not something that we need to avoid or hide under a rug. People have a choice as to whether they will respond to God, ignore Him, or reject His existence; But no one should seek to hide the possibility of God or fail to examine the result when one begins with God in the learning process. In a pluralistic society, there is room for God and for people who put the value of others ahead of their own self-interests or gratification. God is in the workplace as well as in a church or a synagogue.

LEARNING BY DOING HELPS US TO APPRECIATE THE SPILLS IN THE KITCHEN

Learning is not just a process of correcting or repairing deficiencies. We hire and promote people for what they can do, not for what they cannot do. As people learn, we should encourage them to develop their gifts and maximize their strengths. Learning in the work environment should include elbow room for mistakes. In the absence of grace, there will be no reaching for potential.

When we remodeled our headquarters building a few years ago, my colleague Sandy Jett was given the job of making everybody happy and also bringing the new construction in on budget. It was a challenging and frustrating job. We had developed an innovative design to accommodate the change we were making in the way people would work together, and we were also adding new office technology. The prices we had originally received from the contractor turned out to be far too conservative.

Sandy was used to delivering what he had promised, and this time it was not going to happen. We had to go to the board for authorization to spend more money. Sandy and I had both made some mistakes and errors in judgment. He needed encouragement and shade with

our board of directors. Sandy and I made the presentation to the board together, and we received the necessary authorization. He later told me that before the board meeting he was ready to "fire the contractor and jump off a cliff. But," he continued, "what could have been the lowest point in my career turned out to be one of the high points because of the encouragement and support you gave me." What I didn't tell him was that, if we hadn't gotten the authorization, I was going to jump off the cliff with him!

As we work with people and give them big jobs to do, we must recognize the tendency we have to remember the bad and overlook the potential. In examining the potential of individuals, we must focus on their strengths and not just their mistakes. We cannot be limited by what they may have spilled in the kitchen.

The potential of the new also requires testing and piloting. Successful new businesses are never developed on the drawing board or in market analysis or focus study groups. The successful business must be piloted and tested. Ken Hansen, our former chairman, has reminded us that "if a thing is worth doing, it is worth doing poorly to begin with." In other words, get started, get your hands in the bucket, and understand the theory in a practical application. Soon the time will run out, and if the business is still operated poorly, bury it. But it is important for every learning organization to get that new thing off the drawing board, to get hands-on, and to learn from experience. Too often new ideas are studied and analyzed until they are suffocated.

One aspect of our change from a corporation to a partnership form of organization vividly demonstrates this principle. Under corporate form, shareholders received a short tax form (1099) each year showing the amount of taxable dividends. They only had to enter that number in one place on their tax return. But under partnership form, we had to issue a "K1," which can be a very complicated document. The first K1 we sent out in 1987 required two mailings to shareholders, was more than twenty pages long, and necessitated individual taxpayers to make as many as ten different entries on six different forms. We knew that was not acceptable in the long term. Bruce Duncan and his tax team kept working on improving the process. Last year our K1s had only two numbers to be entered on the tax return, and Bruce is still working on getting that to just one entry. Had we waited until we had resolved this issue, we would never have been able to accomplish the major benefit of partnership form for our shareholders—which has been measured by some to be over one billion dollars. Thanks, Bruce, for getting your hands in the bucket.

It is not always what we know or analyze *before* we make a decision that makes it a great decision. It is what we do *after* we make the decision to implement and execute it that makes it a good decision. More than thirty-five years ago Judy and I made a decision to get married. We thought we knew a lot about each other, but we really didn't. We knew we were attracted to each other, but we did not understand what it was going to be like for the two of us to live together and build a family. What has made it a great decision and a great marriage is not what we knew ahead of time, but what we have done since we made the decision.

MORE TO LEARN AND MORE TO ENJOY

ONE OF THE challenges of learning in business is that people want to be entertained. Old methods of teaching just will not work anymore. If you put a group of workers in a room and lecture to them for four hours, they will turn you off and fail to learn.

Television has conditioned us to expect a certain degree of entertainment and sensational visual effects as part of the communication process. It has also resulted in shorter attention spans and has encouraged most of us to attempt to do at least two things at once during the listening process. Many times people are not learning because they are bored. But education can be fun and stimulating, provided we incorporate entertainment in the learning process and catch the student's attention.

For today's audiences with shorter attention-spans, videos, CD-ROMs, the computer, interactive compact disks (CDIs), and other technologies can make the transfer of information more powerful and effective. For example, Service-Master has recently prepared a series of CDIs containing short discussion clips by leaders of ServiceMaster as they share their views on our company objectives and on our twenty-one principles of leadership. Our size and diversity of locations means that it may be the only way for some of us to touch and communicate with managers in many locations.

Information is a source of learning. But unless it is organized, processed, and available to the right people in a format for decision making, it is a burden, not a benefit. It is just data, not information. In some cases, we are still using and designing information to flow upstream so that top management can control the organization. But why can't we look at information as something that should flow the natural way—downstream. Shouldn't it flow down from a common database to help the front-line managers make good decisions? What information do they need to get the job done? This query should be the fundamental inquiry for information planning in the firm. Information flow should be reviewed continually, tracing the decision-making process

and the various transactions that support the delivery of the product or service to the customer. Too much of the work of middle managers today is simply to pass information up and down. As we said before, with each relay switch or layer of management, you double the noise and cut the power in half.

WE LEARN AS WE PARTICIPATE

People want greater participation in decisions that affect their welfare and their future. This is true not only in the work environment, but also in our schools.

Several years ago I had the opportunity to visit one of our education customers. As I was touring a grade-school facility with the principal, a third-grade student came up to her and asked when she could become a member of the student committee that was reviewing teacher performance. What will be her expectation of participation when she joins the work force? Will we be prepared for her? What information will she need? What will motivate her to be excited about a continuing learning process? How will her potential be fully developed? The firm needs people who can think, make judgments, and be accountable and responsible for their actions. The coming generations will want even more to say about their work environment.

Today ServiceMaster serves over six

million homeowners. We have some understanding of why our customers buy and continue to buy. But we are always learning and also seeking to learn from the coming generation of buyers. How do we prepare for their buying patterns? Our marketing efforts must become a continuum of learning and listening.

Paul Bert heads up this effort and has developed many of our innovative marketing and sales methods, including our easy access point for all of our Consumer Services—1-800-WE SERVE. He has called our attention to the importance of listening and learning from school children as we try to understand both our present and future customers. They are influencing their parents' decisions and are developing strong views about the home of the future—what they want and what they need. Paul and his team keep us thinking about the future. Not all their ideas and conclusions will work. As they learn and think a step or a mile ahead of the rest of us in the firm, they must also think and relate to the needs and necessities of the present. It is a challenge for good and fertile minds.

A Partnership That Extends Beyond the Firm

As the firm recognizes its responsibility for the continuous learning process, it should be involved in supporting and cooperating with other learning organiza-

tions. This includes our traditional education system, which is facing several perplexing challenges. Issues such as the dropout rate or the at-risk child and lack of parental support or inadequate resources have the potential to impose unacceptable barriers to lifelong learning. As we increasingly move to an information-based society and a global marketplace, such barriers will create a growing gap between the "haves" and "have nots." It could have an even greater economic implication if it results in a scarcity of qualified labor necessary to maintain a competitive edge in the world market.

To resolve this growing predicament, those in the marketplace must recognize the need to encourage learning and to develop partnerships between the firm of the school and the firm of the business. The business firm is a customer of the school. It can provide more than tax dollars or contributions. It can provide work and a vehicle to apply what has been learned so that the student can make a valuable contribution to others. Curriculums should not be developed without the firm's active involvement. Together, the school and the business firm must respond to the challenge of providing a continuum of learning that included dropouts or at-risk children so that they too can have lives of improvement, productivity, and dignity.

Our firm has developed a number of these partnerships. They include financial support for the purchase of computer, scientific, and athletic equipment. But even more important to the students and people of our firm, they include the opportunity for active involvement of our employees in the learning and mentoring process as they tutor and relate to the students. The benefits of such a partnership are mutual and long lasting. For the most part, these programs have been developed by our employees under the leadership of Wally Duzansky and many others and have been recognized for their effectiveness, including being designated as one of President Bush's Thousand Points of Light.

The firm is part of the continuum of learning. For all of us—students, teachers, workers, mentors, servants, and leaders learning *is* a lifelong experience.

Chuck Swindoll was taking stock of the attitudes of Americans, and he couldn't help but notice a disturbing reality: People settle. When they could be great, they accept being good—or perhaps just being "OK." When they could shine like the brightest star, they opt to put forth only enough energy for the required soft glow. They settle.

Worse, this acceptance of mediocrity is just as common among followers of Christ—perhaps more common—as it is among unbelievers. Swindoll began to wonder: As believers in the God of the universe—the God that defines perfection—shouldn't we soar like eagles instead of crawling like worms?

Writing from his theological background but in his down-to-earth style, Swindoll penned *Living Above the Level of Mediocrity* in 1987 to inspire and challenge believers to take flight. And nowhere is it more important to "live differently" (as Swindoll puts it) than at work—where our skills, or our lack of skills, are constantly on display.

Swindoll, who since 1994 has served as president of Dallas Theological Seminary, writes that making the jump from an intellectual understanding to living differently comes down to four things—vision, determination, priorities, and accountability.

This chapter outlines those four factors, but focuses primarily on vision as a tool for helping us live above the level of mediocrity. Swindoll includes in the chapter his "ABCs" of vision—a list of five attributes of a person of vision.

To make his point, Swindoll uses the Old Testament story of the twelve Hebrew spies who were sent to check out the Promised Land. This story, found in Numbers 13, illustrates the power of negative thinking and the value of courage. Ten of the spies said that the people of Israel would be slaughtered by the inhabitants of the Promised Land. But two, Caleb and Joshua, stood against the wave of popular opinion.

"With vision," Swindoll notes, "there is no room to be frightened. No reason for intimidation."

Joshua's vision was based in his faith in the power of God. His faith led to vision, and his vision ultimately led to his leadership of the Children of Israel into the Promised Land. A life of faith ought to yield vision that pushes us beyond mediocrity and an internal attitude that sets us apart as leaders.

With vision, we take the first step out of mediocrity; and before we know it, we're soaring with the eagles.

9 Vision: Seeing Beyond the Majority

from *Living Above the Level of Mediocrity* by Charles R. Swindoll

Editors' note: Swindoll spends the first four chapters of Living Above the Level of Mediocrity *stressing the importance of thinking clearly—that everything we deal with in life begins in the mind. In this chapter, he builds upon that foundation by exploring the relationship of vision.*

HAVING COME TO terms with the importance of thinking clearly, we are ready to tackle the second challenge: *living differently*. Whoever clears away the mental fog is no longer satisfied drifting along with the masses. *Vision* replaces mental resistance. *Determination* marches in, overstepping laziness and indifference. And it's then that we begin to realize the value of *priorities*, a step which dictates the need for personal *accountability*. I will define each of these four terms a little later. But for now, consider them as one domino bumping the next. Each one of these stages precedes the next, forming a unit that spells out the basics of living differently—with excellence—in a world of sameness, boredom, and futility.

By "world" I mean the invisible yet surrounding atmosphere in which we live that "erodes faith, dissipates hope, and corrupts love," as Eugene Peterson puts it. It may be a system of thought that includes human intelligence, persuasive winsomeness, clever and appealing logic, competition, creativity, and resourcefulness, but it lacks the essential ingredients that enable us to soar like an eagle. The most treacherous part of all is the way we become brainwashed by the system, thus blocked from reaching our full potential. The end result is predictable: internal anxiety and external mediocrity.

THREE INDISPUTABLE FACTS ABOUT THE WORLD SYSTEM

Let's go a little deeper into an understanding of the world system. To give ourselves a point of reference, let's look again at Jesus' words. Pay close attention to His repeated remarks about being anxious.

"No one can serve two masters; for either he will hate the one and love the other, or he will hold to one and despise the other. You cannot serve God and mammon. For this reason I say to you, do not be anxious for your life, as to what you shall eat, or what you shall drink; nor for your body, as to what you shall put on. Is not life more than food, and the body than clothing? Look at the birds of the air, that they do not sow, neither do they reap, nor gather into barns, and yet your heavenly Father feeds them. Are you not worth much more than they? And which of you by being anxious can add a single cubit to his life's span? And why are you anxious about clothing? Observe how the lilies of the field grow; they do not toil nor do they spin, yet I say to you that even Solomon in all his glory did not clothe himself like one of these. But if God so arrays the grass of the field, which is alive today and tomorrow is thrown into the furnace, will He not much more do so for you, O men of little faith? Do not be anxious then, saying, 'What shall we eat?' or 'What shall we drink?' or 'With what shall we clothe ourselves?' For all these things the Gentiles eagerly seek; for your heavenly Father knows that you need all these things. But seek first His kingdom and His righteousness; and all these things shall be added to you. Therefore do not be anxious for tomorrow; for tomorrow will care for itself. Each day has enough trouble of its own." (Matt. 6:24-34)

I never read those familiar words without becoming aware of the difference between the way people *naturally* live (full of worry and anxiety) and the way our Lord planned for us to live (free of all that excess baggage). Then why? Why do we opt for a lifestyle that is the very antithesis of what He designed for us? Because the "system" sucks us in! We yield to a lesser lifestyle because "all those things the Gentiles eagerly seek" (v. 32) occupy our attention and ultimately dominate our lives. As I see it, there are three interrelated factors.

1. We live in a negative, hostile world. Face it, my friend, the system that surrounds us focuses on the negatives: what is wrong, not what is right; what is missing, not what is present; what is ugly, not what is beautiful; what is destructive, not what is constructive; what cannot be done, not what can be done; what hurts, not what helps; what we lack, not what we have. You question that? Pick up your local newspaper and read it through. See if the majority of the news doesn't concern itself (and the reader) with the negatives. It's contagious!

This negative mindset leads to incredible feelings of anxiety. Surround most people with enough negatives and I can guarantee the result: fear, resentment, and anger. Negative information plus hostile thinking equals anxiety. And yet Jesus said again and again, "Don't be anxious." The world system, I repeat, works directly against the life God planned for His people. The realization of this led Isaac Watts, over 250 years ago, to write:

> Are there no foes for me to face?
> Must I not stem the flood?
> Is this vile world a friend to grace
> To help me on to God?

2. We are engulfed in mediocrity and cynicism (a direct result of living in a negative world). Without the motivation of divinely empowered insight and enthusiasm, people tend toward the average, doing just enough to get by. Thus, the fallout from the system is mediocrity. The majority dictates the rules, and excitement is replaced with a shrug of the shoulders. Excellence is not only lost in the shuffles whenever it rears its head, it is considered a threat.

3. Most choose not to live differently. Those who take their cues from the system blend into the drab backdrop of the majority. Words like "Just go with the flow" and "Don't make waves" and "Who cares?" begin to gain a hearing.

Stop and think. In a world where all that cynicism is present, what is absent? Courage! That strong muscle of character that gives a nation its pride and gives a home its purpose and gives a person the will to excel is gone. I'm certainly not the first to point out the danger of a lack of courage. Aleksandr Solzhenitsyn's speeches frequently include such warnings:

Must one point out that from ancient times a decline in courage has been considered the beginning of the end?

What, then, does it take to live differently? When I think of *vision*, I have in mind the ability to see above and beyond the majority. Again I am reminded of the eagle, which has eight times as many visual cells per cubic centimeter than does a human. This translates into rather astounding abilities. For example, flying at 600 feet elevation, an eagle can spot an object the size of a dime moving through six-inch grass. The same creature can see three-inch fish jumping in a lake five miles away. Eaglelike people can envision what most would miss.

By determination, I think of inner fortitude, strength of character—being disciplined to remain consistent, strong, and diligent regardless of the odds or the demands. Again, the eagle represents this trait. Bald eagles are adamant in the defense of their territory and their young. The strength in the eagle's claws is nothing short of phenomenal—sufficient to grasp and break large bones in a man's forearm. Eagle types possess tenacity.

The other two are virtually self-explanatory. *Priorities* have to do with choosing first things first—doing essential things in the order of importance, bypassing the incidentals. And *accountability* relates to answering the hard questions, being closely in touch with a few individuals rather than living like an isolated Lone Ranger. Eaglelike folks may be rare, but they possess an incredible loyalty when they do link up.

For the remainder of this chapter, let's concentrate on the value of vision.

TWO COURAGEOUS MEN
WHO DISAGREED WITH THE MAJORITY

The best way I know to stimulate you toward a renewed commitment to excellence is to return to Scripture for an inspired account. The one I have in mind is tucked away in the fourth book of the Old Testament, the Book of Numbers, chapter 13.

Some Background

Five things should be remembered in order for us to be brought up to speed here in Numbers 13.

First, there has been an exodus. The Israelites have been set free from Egyptian bondage. Pharaoh has let the people go. They have departed from Egypt with all their belongings and with all their family members.

Second, under Moses' leadership God's chosen people have arrived at the edge of the Promised Land. According to the last verse of chapter 12, "the people . . . camped in the wilderness of Paran," right at the edge of Canaan (the Promised Land). In the exodus God showed Himself strong. He displayed His miraculous power when the Israelites went through the Red Sea and

when He directed them safely across the wilderness to the land of Canaan. When they arrived at the border, the Israelites could see smoke rising from the cities in the misty distance. Perhaps from that vantage point they could even see some of the walls that surrounded the larger cities. I'm sure their hearts beat faster as they expressed their relief and excitement: "Finally . . . we made it!"

Third, the new territory was theirs to claim. God promised it to them.

> "Send out for yourself men so that they may spy out the land of Canaan, which I am going to give to the sons of Israel; you shall send a man from each of their fathers' tribes, every one a leader among them"

God clearly promised His people the land. "You'll have to invade it and fight, but I promise you that victory is *guaranteed.*" Nobody on this earth ever had a better deal in battle than those people!

When General Dwight Eisenhower and his brain trust were about to lead our troops through the Normandy Invasion back in World War II, they were filled with anxiety brought on by uncertainty. And anxiety increased when the weather worsened. "Shall we proceed? Shall we wait? Shall we abort the mission entirely?" We can hardly imagine the churning uneasiness. And even though Eisenhower had this massive assault ready to move into operation, he wasn't sure that the troops could make a safe landing, to say nothing of what they might encounter from the enemy forces. Finally, with anxious uncertainty, the general signaled thumbs up.

The Israelites faced nothing like that. They had the sure promise of God. "You will have the land." No troops ever had greater reason to fight with assurance.

Fourth, God commanded Moses to spy out the land. In order to plan an intelligent battle strategy, he was to send in a few selected scouts to spy out the land. So Moses cooperated. Remember this: Not once were the spies asked to give their opinion about whether they could take the land. No need for that since God had already promised. Instead they were told precisely what to do.

So Moses sent them from the wilderness of Paran at the command of the Lord, all of them men who were heads of the sons of Israel. These then were their names: from the tribe of Reuben, Shammua the son of Zaccur; from the tribe of Simeon, Shaphat the son of Hori; from the tribe of Judah, Caleb the son of Jephunneh; from the tribe of Issachar, Igal the son of Joseph; from the tribe of Ephraim, Hoshea the son of Nun; from the tribe of Benjamin, Palti the son of Raphu; from the tribe of Zebulun, Gaddiel the son of Sodi; from the tribe of Joseph, from the tribe of Manasseh, Gaddi the son of Susi; from the tribe of Dan, Ammiel the son of Gemalli; from

the tribe of Asher, Sethur the son of Michael; from the tribe of Naphtali, Nahbi the son of Vophsi; from the tribe of Gad, Geuel the son of Machi. These are the names of the men whom Moses sent to spy out the land; but Moses called Hoshea the son of Nun, Joshua (vv. 3-16).

Back in those days each one of those names was familiar. They were like twelve famous mayors in America today, or twelve of our more prominent governors or senators. They were famous men among the Israelites. I emphasize that point because I don't want you to think for a moment that some of those men were over-the-hill-type guys, lacking good sense. All twelve were leader types, but only two soared above the restrictive mindset so common in the system.

Fifth, their assignment was clear. Painfully, explicitly clear.

When Moses sent them to spy out the land of Canaan, he said to them, "Go up there into the Negev; then go up into the hill country. And see what the land is like, and whether the people who live in it are strong or weak, whether they are few or many. And how is the land in which they live, is it good or bad? And how are the cities in which they live, are they like open camps or with fortifications? And how is the land, is it fat or lean? Are there trees in it or not? Make an effort then to get some of the fruit of the land . . ." (vv. 17–20).

End of assignment. Once they found out those things, mission accomplished! Never once does Moses say, "And when you return, advise us on whether we ought to invade the land." No, that wasn't their mandate. They were told to scope out the land, to do a quick, secret reconnaissance, and to come back with a report about what they had observed.

The spies left and stayed gone for forty days.

So they went up and spied out the land from the wilderness of Zin as far as Rehob, at Lebo-hamath. When they had gone up into the Negev, they came to Hebron where Ahiman, Sheshai and Talmai, the descendants of Anak were. (Now Hebron was built seven years before Zoan in Egypt.) Then they came to the valley of Eshcol and from there cut down a branch with a single cluster of grapes; and they carried it on a pole between two men, with some of the pomegranates and the figs. That place was called the valley of Eshcol, because of the cluster which the sons of Israel cut down from there.

When they returned from spying out the land, at the end of forty days, they proceeded to come to Moses and Aaron and to all the congregation of the sons of Israel in the wilderness of Paran, at Kadesh; and they brought back word to them and to all the congregation and showed them the fruit of the land. Thus they told him, and said, "We went in to the land where you sent us; and it certainly does flow with milk and honey, and this is its fruit" (vv. 21–27).

While these twelve men were in the land of Canaan, they took samples of the fruit and brought them back. Once they returned to the Israelite camp, they displayed the grapes and showed them the fruit of the land. And all the people gathered around and listened as the report was given. So far so good. Beautiful fruit. Delicious. Impressive report. I'm sure there were a few oohs and aahs.

NEGATIVE REPORT

But while everyone was getting excited, ten of the spies went on:

"Nevertheless, the people who live in the land are strong, and the cities are fortified and very large; and moreover, we saw the descendants of Anak there. Amalek is living in the land of the Negev and the Hittites and the Jebusites and the Amorites are living in the hill country, and the Canaanites are living by the sea and by the side of the Jordan.

"We are not able to go up against the people, for they are too strong for us" (vv. 28–29, 31).

I find myself wanting to shout back, "Hey, wait a minute! Who asked you? Nobody wants to know if we're able to go up or not. That wasn't your assignment, men. God has already promised us that it is our land. We just want to know what the land is like."

Notice that these ten men went far beyond their assignment.

> So they gave out to the sons of Israel a bad report of the land which they had spied out, saying, "The land through which we have gone, in spying it out, is a land that devours its inhabitants; and all the people whom we saw in it are men of great size. There also we saw the Nephilim (the sons of Anak are part of the Nephilim); and we became like grasshoppers in our own sight, and so we were in their sight." (vv. 32–33)

"Wow! You people cannot believe the size of those giants!" Today I suppose we would say, "They looked like professional athletes!"

Ever been at courtside at a professional basketball game? If you have, then you know what it is like to be around people who make you feel like a grasshopper. I distinctly recall standing alongside the Los Angeles Lakers center, Kareem Abdul-Jabbar. We're talking, "Chuck, the grasshopper."

I have spoken at several professional football pre-game chapel services. And invariably, I feel as if I am surrounded by giants! One time, most of the men were sitting on one side of the room. I asked if some would mind moving to the other side, since the room was beginning to sink on that side. When they began to move about, I definitely felt like an insect. I just hoped one of them wouldn't step on me as they lumbered out the door after the service. That's bound to be how those spies felt back in Moses' day.

Now what kind of impact did this narrow vision have on the people? Just in case you wonder if negativism and restrictive vision are contagious, keep reading:

> Then all the congregation lifted up their voices and cried, and the people wept that night. And all the sons of Israel grumbled against Moses and Aaron; and the whole congregation said to them, "Would that we had died in the land of Egypt! Or would that we had died in this wilderness!" (Num. 14:1–2)

You say, "How could they ever say such a thing? God *promised* they would have the land!" Because negativism is infectious. Because lack of vision from the world system engulfs us. Human reasoning overrules faith! Natural thinking says you can't whip people that big. You can't win if you invade that land. I mean, look at how many there are! Count them: There are the Jebusites and the Hittites and the Amorites and the Canaanites—

probably even "the termites." *Everybody* in the land is against this wandering band of Hebrews! And add to that list the sons of Anak, the giants! Can't you just hear those Israelites, "We've got to face the giants!" When you think like that, it's retreat city!

> So they said to one another, "Let us appoint a leader and return to Egypt." (v. 4)

There's always some guy who has a creative idea like "Let's retreat! Let's go back. Too formidable!" You wonder what impact it had on Moses and Aaron?

> Then Moses and Aaron fell on their faces in the presence of all the assembly of the congregation of the sons of Israel. (v. 5)

When the majority lack vision, their shortsightedness tends to take a severe toll on those trying to lead.

Positive Report . . . Unlimited Vision

Now the good news *is* that those ten spies were not the only ones who gave a report. I have purposely left out two courageous men until now. One is named *Caleb*.

> Then Caleb quieted the people before Moses, and said, "We should by all means go up and take possession of it,

for we shall surely overcome it." (13:30) The other is named *Joshua*.

> And Joshua the son of Nun and Caleb the son of Jephunneh, of those who had spied out the land, tore their clothes (14:6).

Both men ripped their garments when they saw Moses and Aaron on their faces and said, "Wait a minute! There's another side to all this. In fact, there is an issue at stake. It's time for us to be courageous. Let's start seeing this challenge through eyes of faith!"

> And they spoke to all the congregation of the sons of Israel, saying, "The land which we passed through to spy out is an exceedingly good land. If the Lord is pleased with us, then He will bring us into this land, and give it to us—a land which flows with milk and honey. Only do not rebel against the Lord; and do not fear the people of the land, for they shall be our prey. Their protection has been removed from them, and the Lord is with us; do not fear them" (vv. 7–9).

I love those courageous words. They always remind me of the opening lines of Psalm 27:

> The Lord is my light and my salvation;
> Whom shall I fear?

The Lord is the defense of my life;
Whom shall I dread?
When evildoers came upon me to
devour my flesh,
My adversaries and my enemies, they
stumbled and fell.
Though a host encamp against me,
My heart will not fear,
Though war arise against me,
In spite of this I shall be confident.
(vv. 1–3)

With vision there is no room to be frightened. No reason for intimidation. It's time to march forward! Let's be confident and positive! And after a Caleb-Joshua speech, people are ready to applaud and say, "Good job. Let's go!" Right?

Wrong—look for yourself. "But all the congregation said to stone them with stones" (Num. 14:10). Which tells you what people think of positive thinking. Here are two men God smiled upon. Two men Solzhenitsyn would have been proud of. Two men you and I admire, men of rare vision. But the majority said, "They're out to lunch. They're wrong. We can't possibly stand against such obstacles." This kind of majority attitude reminds me of a quote by Arnold Toynbee that goes something like this: "It is doubtful if the majority has *ever* been right." Those words always make me smile.

ONE QUALITY ESSENTIAL FOR UNIQUENESS

Now, we are not studying ancient history. We're thinking about living today. My interest isn't in writing a book that traces the Hebrews from Paran into Canaan. I'm far more interested in helping people like us to cope with and conquer today's obstacles. And they are nonetheless formidable. If you told a group of people that giants stand against you, without hesitation most folks would say, "Give up now, surrender, quit." Enter: anxiety. Exit: peace. But since when do people of faith conduct their lives on the basis of sight?

Did you observe something conspicuously absent from that story? The first thing that goes when you imbibe the system is courageous vision. Vision—the one essential ingredient for being an original in a day of copies gets lost, overwhelmed by the odds. Too bad! We start focusing on the trouble. We start numbering the people. We start measuring their height and weighing them in. Then we start comparing the odds. The result is predictable: We become intimidated and wind up *defeated*.

What is your Canaan? What is your challenge? Which giants make you feel like a grasshopper when you face them? What does your future resemble when you measure it on the basis of facts and figures? You'd like not to surrender, right?

You'd like to be courageous, wouldn't you? There is a way through, but you'll need one essential quality—vision.

Vision is the ability to see God's presence, to perceive God's power, to focus on God's plan in spite of the obstacles.

I sometimes like to spell out things in A-B-C fashion. So let's close this chapter with an "alphabet" of vision—A-B-C-D-E.

A. *Attitude.* When you have vision it affects your attitude. Your attitude is optimistic rather than pessimistic. Your attitude stays positive rather than negative. Not foolishly positive, as though in fantasy, for you are reading God into your circumstances. So when a situation comes that cuts your feet out from under you, you don't throw up your arms and panic. You don't give up. Instead, you say, "Lord, this is Your moment. This is where You take charge. You're in this." Caleb and Joshua came back, having seen the same obstacles the other ten spies saw, but they had a different attitude. Remember their words? "We are well able to handle it." So are you, my friend.

B. *Belief:* This is nothing more than having a strong belief in the power of God; having confidence in others around you who are in similar battles with you; and, yes, having confidence in yourself, by the grace of God. Refusing to give in to temptation, cynicism, and doubt. Not allowing yourself to become a jaded individual. Belief in oneself is terribly important.

People need an atmosphere in which they can specialize, hone their skills, and discover their distinctiveness. The biographies of the great are sprinkled with accounts of how some teacher or some kindly employer looked closely enough to see a spark no one else saw and for periods, at least, believed in their ability to perfect that gift when no one else did. The Taft family . . . was evidently good at pushing their children to cut their own swath and to find a specialty of which to be proud. When Martha Taft was in elementary school in Cincinnati she was asked to introduce herself. She said, "My name is Martha Bowers Taft. My great-grandfather was President of the United States. My grandfather was United States senator. My daddy is ambassador to Ireland. And I am a Brownie."

C. *Capacity.* What I have in mind here is a willingness to be stretched. When God has you look at your Canaan with all its formidable foes, He says, in effect, "You must be willing to be stretched. You have to allow your capacity to be invaded by My power.

I like what William James wrote:

> Everyone knows on any given day that there are energies slumbering in him which the incitements of that day do not call forth. . . . Compared with what we ought to be, we are only half awake. Our fires are damped, our drafts are checked. We are making use of only a

small part of our possible mental and physical resources. . . . Stating the thing broadly, the human individual thus lives far within his limits; he possesses powers of various sorts he habitually fails to use.

Isn't that the truth! Alleged "impossibilities" are opportunities for our capacities to be stretched.

D. *Determination.* Determination is hanging tough when the going gets rough. I have no magic wand to wave over your future and say, "All of a sudden everything is going to fall into place." Vision requires determination, a constant focus on God who is watching and smiling.

E. *Enthusiasm.* Great word, *enthusiasm.* Its Greek origin is *éntheos,* "God in." It is the ability to see God in a situation, which makes the event exciting. And, by the way, do you know that He is Watching? Do you realize that? Something happens to our vision that is almost magical when we become convinced that God our heavenly Father is involved in our activities and is applauding them.

Bob Richards, the Olympic pole vaulter of years ago, loved to tell the story of the goof-off who played around with football. He was somewhere between the bench and off the team. If there was mischief to be done, this kid was doing it. Everything was casual, no big deal. And he added very little to the team. He practiced but he wasn't committed. He had a uniform and would show up to play, but never with enthusiasm.

He liked to hear the cheers, but not to charge the line. He liked to wear the suit, but not to practice. He did not like to put himself out. One day the players were doing fifty laps, and this showpiece was doing his usual five. The coach came over and said, "Hey kid, here is a telegram for you." The kid said, "Read it for me, Coach." He was so lazy he did not even like to read. The coach opened it up and read, "Dear son, your father is dead. Come home immediately." The coach swallowed hard. He said, "Take the rest of the week off." He didn't care if he took the rest of the year off.

Well, funny thing, game time came on Friday and here came the teams rushing out on the field, and lo and behold, the last kid out was the goof-off. No sooner did the gun sound than the kid said, "Coach, can I play today? Can I play?" The coach thought, "Kid you're not playing today. This is homecoming. This is the big game. We need every real guy we have, and you are not one of them." Every time the coach turned around, the kid badgered him: "Coach, please let me play. Coach, I have got to play."

The first quarter ended with the score lopsided against the coach and his team. At half time, they were still further behind. The second half started, and things got progressively worse. The coach, mumbling to himself, began writing out his resignation, and up came the kid. "Coach, Coach, let me play, please!" The coach looked at the scoreboard. "All right," he said, "get in there, kid. You can't hurt anything now."

No sooner did the kid hit the field than his team exploded. He ran, blocked, and tackled like a star. The electricity leaped to the team. The score evened up. In the closing seconds of the game, this kid intercepted a pass and ran all the way for the winning touchdown!

The stands broke loose. The kid was everybody's hero. Such cheering you never heard. Finally the excitement subsided and the coach got over to the kid and said, "I never saw anything like that. What in the world happened to you out there?" He said, "Coach, you know my dad died last week." "Yes," he said, "I read you the telegram." "Well, Coach," he said, "my dad was blind. And today was the first day he ever saw me play."

Today may be the first day you realized that your heavenly Father is watching you in life. He really is not absent, unconcerned, blind, or dead. He is alive. He is watching. He cares. That can make all the difference in the world.

Even in a world that is negative and hostile. Even in a world where the majority says, "We can't," you can. Trust God today. With eyes of faith, get back in the game. Play it with great enthusiasm. It's time to start soaring . . . which is another way of saying it's time to live differently, which starts with seeing beyond the majority.

The word is *vision*.

PART FOUR
Taking the Lead

E-mail is great, phones are wonderful, and letters can be a delight. But there's something special about getting to know a person face-to-face. When we first met Laurie Beth Jones during a round-table discussion in Chicago, it didn't take long for us to discover that there's no gap between the writer and the person. In person and in her writing, she conveys a sense of spirit and a depth that make it easy to see why she's been successful.

Jones helped lift the faith/work category into the mainstream in 1995 when *Jesus CEO* became a national bestseller. It broke through the myth that books on business and faith only sell in niche markets and should be marketed only through faith-based bookstores. Jones was overt about her source for material, and the business world ate it up. The book, and her follow-up efforts, continues to influence the business landscape.

Jesus CEO clusters vignettes under three big umbrellas. They show Jesus, the Omega leader, as one who demonstrates the strength of self-mastery, the strength of action, and the strength of relationship. The Omega leader is Jones's response to conventional typing of Alpha (masculine) and Beta (feminine) leaders.

Jones's theory of Omega leader reminds us that leadership, as explained and illustrated in Scripture, looks different from human models of leadership.

The chapters in *Jesus CEO* are practical, bite-sized nuggets of inspiration. For example, under the strength of self-mastery we see that He stuck to His mission; He believed in Himself; He guarded His energy; He said thank you; He expressed Himself; He was willing to look foolish; He felt a sense of destiny. Under strength of action we see He broke ranks; He branched out; He formed a team; He boiled it down; He was visible; He took His staff in His hand. Under strength of relationships, we see He empowered women; He treated them as equals; He touched the fragile things; He looked out for the little guys; He played with them; He harbored only good will.

Since the chapters of *Jesus CEO* are short, we selected four to include in this book. The first two provide an introduction to frame the context of her book. The other two chapters show how Jesus lived out leadership.

As a culture, we continually look for more leaders to study and evaluate. Jones reminds us that the life of Jesus Christ illustrates hundreds of lessons for today's businessperson. She demonstrates that the Bible has something to say to us on Monday—not just Sunday. It is practical, pointed, and inspiring.

10

Introduction, The Selection Process, He Did Not Kick the Donkey, and He Said Why Not Me?

from *Jesus CEO* by Laurie Beth Jones

PERHAPS YOU HAVE heard about the Alpha management style—the one based on the masculine, authoritative use of power.

Perhaps you have also heard about the Beta management style—the one based on the feminine, cooperative use of power.

I will introduce what I call the Omega management style—the style that incorporates and enhances them both.

Jesus, CEO: Using Ancient Wisdom for Visionary Leadership is based on three simple premises:

1. One person trained twelve human beings who went on to so influence the world that time itself is now recorded as being before (B.C.) or after (A.D.) his existence.

2. This person worked with a staff that was totally human and not divine ... a staff that in spite of illiteracy, questionable backgrounds, fractious feelings, and momentary cowardice went on to accomplish the tasks he trained them to do. They did this for one main reason—to be with him again.

3. His leadership style was intended to be put to use by any of us.

The idea of Jesus as a Chief Executive Officer (CEO) came to me twenty years ago when I was living in the mountains. It struck me at the time that Jesus had many feminine values in management and that his approach with his staff often ran counter to other management styles and techniques I had both witnessed and experienced. As I started my own advertising agency ten years later and began to encounter businesses on many different levels, I was dismayed to find countless "homeless" people in corporations. I, too, often saw invaluable human energy and intelligence untapped and underutilized. I saw multiple examples of corporate abuse, neglect, and violence. I decided to write this book to help turn the tide and to empower people in all layers of leadership to re-*view* the divine excellence in themselves and in those they serve.

I also found it disturbing that nearly all leadership and management books are written by men. Yet women are the fastest-growing segment of business owners in this country. *USA Today* recently reported that soon women will employ more people than all the Fortune 500 companies combined. Similarly, nearly 80 percent of all businesses in the United States employ twenty people or less. Clearly, small groups of people led by innovative leaders and managers make up the strength, and hope, of this nation. With the business world changing so rapidly and so drastically, it seemed to me that we need creative and innovative role models now more than ever before. I believe the world is crying out for leaders whose goals are to build up, not to tear down; to nurture, not to exploit; to undergird and enhance, rather than to dominate. Jesus as a leader struck me as the noblest of them all.

I believe Jesus' "Omega" management style incorporates and transcends the best of the Alpha (masculine) and Beta (feminine) leadership styles, because by harnessing spiritual energy, each of us, female and male, can become the empowered leaders that the next millennium will require.

To those who are looking for tips on how to make a fast buck or get a quick management fix, this book will have little or no relevance. I am searching for people who are willing to plant the fields that lead to the harvest and who recognize that the workplace, where most of us spend the greater part of our lives, is indeed very holy and fertile ground.

THE SELECTION PROCESS

In your humanness, you might hope your new staff will have the powers of angels, but the first one pointed out to you smells not like heavenly phosphorescence but like mud and dead fish.

The next one is not drawn from the halls of a university but is out collecting taxes in the name of the government that everyone hates. The selection process continues. . . . Your staff and followers are plucked from trees, back alleys, and down at the pier.

And as you gaze on your chosen few, you realize that this group will outlive you and must carry out the task you cannot accomplish without them: to change the world. You have three years to train them. What do you do?

This is the question that faced Jesus, a young leader . . . a leader who, like many of us, had to depend on others to accomplish a goal.

In studying Jesus' leadership techniques, I began to realize that he, the original Omega leader, had three categories of strengths:

- the strength of self-mastery
- the strength of action
- the strength of relationships

Currently you may be strong in only one or two of these areas. Yet success in management requires the total combination. For example, a physician who has self-mastery and action skills, but lacks relationship skills, will be limited in her/his career. Likewise, we are all too familiar with the downfall of political leaders who had relationship and action skills, but lacked strength in the area of self-mastery. The goal is to heighten your awareness level in each category and to assist you in the process of mastering them all.

HE DID NOT KICK THE DONKEY

The Old Testament tells a story about the prophet Balaam. He was on a misguided mission to curse someone when his donkey suddenly stopped on the road. No matter how hard the prophet kicked her, she would not budge. Without the donkey, Balaam could not carry out his deed. He proceeded to beat the donkey severely, apparently practicing the management style of ruling through fear and intimidation. Finally the donkey cried out, "Why are you beating me? Haven't I served you faithfully all these years?" An angel spoke to Balaam and said, "You fool, quit beating her. Even she could see I was standing here. Your donkey just saved your life, for if you had carried out this mission you would have been killed. In fact, I would have killed you and let the donkey live." The angel then left, and I can just imagine Balaam kissing the donkey all the way back to the stable.

There is a fine line between knowing when opposition is God trying to show you another way or when it is just a test of courage. If the passively opposing forces cause you to use violence to get them to move, you probably are not on God's path. If you do everything you possibly can to get something to happen, and it doesn't, then an angel must be on the road somewhere, so don't beat the donkey. Take a little time out, smell the flowers, and rethink your route . . . and your mission.

When the Roman guards came to arrest Jesus, Peter sprang to his defense and prepared to engage in massive violence. He actually did cut off one guard's ear. Here was a chance for Jesus to escape, but he knew that the Roman guard was part of the plan. He did not kick the Roman "donkey." He knew it was time.

Bernie Siegel, M.D., shocks his cancer patients when he asks them, "Why did you need this illness?" He claims that our bodies break down to give us a message . . . and many times it is a message that we have been ignoring. According to Dr. Siegel, while nobody wants to be ill, many patients say that cancer was the best thing that ever happened to them. They learned to appreciate life and to express their feelings to their loved ones. They were able to pick up the paintbrush they previously had been too busy to hold. Even illness can be a blessing.

Flat tires that keep us from catching a plane . . . missed appointments that cause a project's delay . . . bankers who tell us no . . . all of these can be donkeys that are keeping us from endangering ourselves in ways we cannot see.

Many times when you feel farthest from the truth, you are very close to it. And when you think you are on top of the world, you can be sitting in a very dangerous place.

When the donkey you are riding suddenly refuses to move, don't kick it. Get off and look for the angel standing in the road. That donkey might be saving your life. (They weren't given big ears for nothing.)

Jesus did not kick the donkey.

Question
Which circumstances in your life remind you most of the balking donkey?

Question
When has a "balking donkey" actually protected you?

HE SAID "WHY NOT ME?"

When something bad happens to us, one of the first thoughts we have is usually "Why me, Lord?" As the old man Tevye moans in the play *Fiddler on the Roof*, "I know we're the Chosen People, God, but can't you choose somebody else part of the time?"

Yet a key ingredient of leadership and maturity is to be able to say "Why not me?" My friend Catherine rolls her eyes when she hears testimonies on television about how God spared someone from a horrible plane crash or a pile-up on the freeway. "Does that mean that God didn't love the people who were in the crash?" she asks incredulously. The very idea that God blesses only the good and punishes only the evil leads immediately to the question "Then what did Jesus do to cause him to die so young and so painfully?" God is much bigger than our understanding of good and bad, and has an eternal plan that none of us grasps totally. In fact, the willingness to enter into whatever God wants is one of the hallmarks of spiritual leadership.

Jesus told the story about a wealthy landowner who entrusted his vineyards to a certain group of people. The landowner sent emissary after emissary to the far country to see how his land was faring, only to have them return with reports of being ignored, mistreated, and even beaten and stoned. At this point I can just see Jesus, as the landowner's eldest son, stepping up and saying "Father, why not send me?"

David also uttered these words when all the other Israelites were trembling in their tents as the giant Goliath boomed out his insults and challenges. "No one else is willing to go out there. Why not me?"

The why-not-me question applies equally to the blessing side of the equation. If you study some of the most successful athletes or entrepreneurs, you will undoubtedly find that at some point they looked at other people who were experiencing success and said "Why not me?"

A year ago my mother went to visit an art gallery in Sedona, Arizona. After Mom oohed and ahhed about how lucky the woman working there was to live in such a hauntingly beautiful part of the country, the woman said, "Why don't you move here?" Mom immediately replied that she didn't think she could afford to live there. The woman laughed and said, "You think I'm made of money? No way. But one day I decided that this is where I wanted to live, so I up and moved here. You can, too." Then she gave her a list of real estate offices to visit. On the way home Mom kept saying to herself "That woman lives in Sedona. Why not me?" She went home to El Paso, praying the whole way, put her home of thirty-four years on the market, sold it that day to a man who had always admired it, and

within sixty days was sipping tea on her new balcony in Sedona.

Lately one of my mental exercises is to look at people who are doing more of what I really want to be doing and realizing "They are doing this. Why not me?" This is not done with envy, jealousy, or malice. Mostly it is about recognizing that none of us is to a caste system born, and that we, too, can delight in the benefits and the banquets of life.

Jesus was in effect a walking invitation to a Great Banquet. And the only requirement for attendance is that the person accept the invitation. "Moses is going. David is going. Queen Esther is going. Jeremiah is going. The whole gang's going to be there. "Why not me?"

Question
Do you often feel envy about someone else's success?

Question
What could *you* do to attain that success?

from the editors of *The Life@Work Journal*

• • •

If poetry is defined as an economy of words that compellingly engages the imagination and succinctly addresses the heart of the matter, then perhaps Max De Pree is a corporate poet.

De Pree was chairman and CEO of Herman Miller Inc. from 1980 to 1987, and he is a lifelong champion of values-based leadership that are rooted in Biblical principles and his faith in Christ. The success of Herman Miller, which for decades has been one of the most respected and profitable furniture manufacturers in America, helped earn De Pree such honors as a spot in *Fortune* magazine's National Business Hall of Fame. But it was his ideas—and his skill in presenting them—that made him a best-selling author in the business world.

His first book, *Leadership is an Art,* was released in 1990 and is considered required reading for any student of leadership. As the title suggests, De Pree focuses on the art of leadership, not the science of leadership that occupies the attention of most would-be gurus. While most leadership books center on what a leader does, this one concentrates on what a leader owes.

It is, De Pree acknowledges, "more a book of ideas than practices." But putting De Pree's ideas into practice allows us to succeed in the art of leadership by "liberating people to do what is required of them in the most effective and humane way possible."

Like *Jesus, CEO,* De Pree shows that the art of leadership, as defined by Scripture, looks different than human-defined models—Scripture-based leadership includes the principal mandate to make a significant difference in the lives of those being led.

In this chapter, De Pree defines leadership in some atypical ways—primarily in terms of stewardship "of assets and legacy, of momentum and effectiveness, of civility and values." Like the rest of the book, this is not a chapter to skim lightly. These are words to reflect upon in the presence of a good cup of coffee that you sip instead of gulp.

Sit back, read slowly, and think hard.

11

What Is Leadership?

from *Leadership is an Art* by Max De Pree

The first responsibility of a leader is to define reality. The last is to say thank you. In between the two, the leader must become a servant and a debtor. That sums up the progress of an artful leader.

Concepts of leadership, ideas about leadership, and leadership practices are the subject of much thought, discussion, writing, teaching, and learning. True leaders are sought after and cultivated. Leadership is not an easy subject to explain. A friend of mine characterizes leaders simply like this: "Leaders don't inflict pain; they bear pain."

The goal of thinking hard about leadership is not to produce great or charismatic or well-known leaders. The measure of leadership is not the quality of the head, but the tone of the body. The signs of outstanding leadership appear primarily among the followers. Are the followers reaching their potential? Are they learning? Serving? Do they achieve the required results? Do they change with grace? Manage conflict?

I would like to ask you to think about the concept of leadership in a certain way. Try to think about a leader, in the words of the gospel writer Luke, as "one who serves." Leadership is a concept of owing certain things to the institution. It is a way of thinking about institutional heirs, a way of thinking about stewardship as contrasted with ownership. Robert Greenleaf has written an excellent book about this idea, *Servant Leadership.*

The art of leadership requires us to think about the leader-as-steward in terms of relationships: of assets and legacy, of momentum and effectiveness, of civility and values.

Leaders should leave behind them assets and a legacy. First, consider assets; certainly leaders owe assets. Leaders owe their institutions vital financial health, and the relationships and reputation that enable continuity of that financial health. Leaders must deliver to their organizations the appropriate services, products, tools, and equipment that people in the organization need in order to be accountable. In many institutions leaders are responsible for providing land and facilities.

But what else do leaders owe? What are artful leaders responsible for? Surely we need to include people. People are the heart and spirit of all that counts. Without people, there is no need for leaders. Leaders can decide to be primarily concerned with leaving assets to their institutional heirs or they can go beyond that and capitalize on the opportunity to leave a legacy, a legacy that takes into account the more difficult, qualitative side of life, one which provides greater meaning, more challenge, and more joy in the lives of those whom leaders enable.

Besides owing assets to their institutions, leaders owe the people in those institutions certain things. Leaders need to be concerned with the institutional value system which, after all, leads to the principles and standards that guide the practices of the people in the institution. Leaders owe a clear statement of the values of the organization. These values should be broadly understood and agreed to and should shape our corporate and individual behavior. What is this value system based on? How is it expressed? How is it audited? These are not easy questions to deal with.

Leaders owe people space, space in the sense of freedom. Freedom in the sense of enabling our gifts to be exercised. We need to give each other the space to grow, to be ourselves, to exercise our diversity. We need to give each other space so that we may both give and receive such beautiful things as ideas, openness, dignity, joy, healing, and inclusion. And in giving each other the gift of space, we need also to offer the gifts of grace and beauty to which each of us is entitled.

Another way to think about what leaders owe is to ask this question: What is it without which this institution would not be what it is?

Leaders are obligated to provide and maintain momentum. Leadership comes with a lot of debts to the future. There are more immediate obligations as well. Momentum is one. Momentum in a vital company is palpable. It is not abstract or mysterious. It is the feeling among a group of people that their lives and work are intertwined and moving toward a recognizable and legitimate goal. It begins with competent leadership and a management team strongly dedicated to aggressive managerial development and opportunities. This team's job is to provide an environment that allows momentum to gather.

Momentum comes from a clear vision of what the corporation ought to be, from a well-thought-out strategy to achieve that vision, and from carefully conceived and communicated directions and plans that enable everyone to participate and be publicly accountable in achieving those plans.

Momentum depends on a pertinent but flexible research and development program led by people with outstanding gifts and unique talents. Momentum results when a corporation has an aggressive, professional, inspired group of people in its marketing and sales units. Momentum results when the operations group serves its customers in such a way that the customer sees them as their best supplier of tools, equipment, and services. Underlying these complex activities is the essential role of the financial team. They provide the financial guidelines and the necessary ratios. They are responsible for equity among the various groups that compose the corporate family.

Leaders are responsible for effectiveness. Much has been written about effectiveness—some of the best of it by Peter Drucker. He has such a great ability to simplify concepts. One of the things he tells us is that efficiency is doing the thing right, but effectiveness is doing the right thing.

Leaders can delegate efficiency, but they must deal personally with effectiveness. Of course, the natural question is "how." We could fill many pages dealing with how to be effective, but I would like to touch on just two ways.

The first is the understanding that effectiveness comes about through enabling others to reach their potential—both their personal potential and their corporate or institutional potential.

In some South Pacific cultures, a speaker holds a conch shell as a symbol of a temporary position of authority. Leaders must understand who holds the conch—that is, who should be listened to and when. This makes it possible for people to use their gifts to the fullest for the benefit of everyone.

Sometimes, to be sure, a leader must choose who is to speak. That is part of the risk of leadership. A leader must assess capability. A leader must be a judge of people. For leaders choose a person, not a position.

Another way to improve effectiveness is to encourage roving leadership. Roving leadership arises and expresses itself at varying times and in varying situations, according to the dictates of those situations. Roving leaders have the special gifts or the special strengths or the special temperament to lead in these special situations. They are acknowledged by others who are ready to follow them.

Leaders must take a role in developing, expressing, and defending civility and values. In a civilized institution or corporation, we see good manners, respect for persons, an understanding of "good goods," and an appreciation of the way in which we serve each other.

Civility has to do with identifying values as opposed to following fashions. Civility might be defined as an ability to distinguish between what is actually healthy and what merely appears to be living. A leader can tell the difference between living edges and dying ones.

To lose sight of the beauty of ideas and of hope and opportunity, and to frustrate the right to be needed, is to be at the dying edge.

To be a part of a throwaway mentality that discards goods and ideas, that discards principles and law, that discards persons and families, is to be at the dying edge.

To be at the leading edge of consumption, affluence, and instant gratification is to be at the dying edge.

To ignore the dignity of work and the elegance of simplicity, and the essential responsibility of serving each other, is to be at the dying edge.

Justice Oliver Wendell Holmes is reported to have said this about simplicity: "I would not give a fig for the simplicity this side of complexity, but I would give my life for the simplicity on the other side of complexity." To be at the living edge is to search out the "simplicity on the other side of complexity."

In a day when so much energy seems to be spent on maintenance and manuals, on bureaucracy and meaningless quantification, to be a leader is to enjoy the special privileges of complexity, of ambiguity, of diversity. But to be a leader means, especially, having the opportunity to make a meaningful difference in the lives of those who permit leaders to lead.

from the editors of *The Life@Work Journal*

. . .

As a young pastor in the 1970s, John Maxwell was struck by the overwhelming importance of effective leadership to the health of a church. Without it, churches died or became stale and had little positive impact. With it, churches thrived, changing individual lives and, as a result, entire communities.

So Maxwell set out on what's become a lifelong study of leadership. And the more he learned, the more he felt compelled to share that knowledge with other pastors. He began writing books, leading seminars, and speaking at conferences. His skills as a motivational speaker and writer combined with his ability to present information in practical and memorable forms quickly made him a hit with other students of leadership—and not just pastors.

Maxwell's messages on leadership have been directed primarily at the clergy, but they apply to everyone with leadership responsibilities (or aspirations), regardless of the structure of their organization. In part, by striking a chord with the business audience, Maxwell's books became bestsellers all across the globe.

In the introduction to *Developing the Leader Within You,* published in 1991, Maxwell states categorically that "everything rises and falls on leadership." Not *almost everything.* Everything. Thus, your level of success—and the level of success of those around you— is determined by the level of your leadership skills.

And while some people are "born leaders," Maxwell contends that leadership as a skill is developed, not discovered. "The truly 'born leader' will always emerge; but, to stay on top, natural leadership characteristics must be developed."

This book lays out a plan for developing leadership skills, and this particular chapter explores one of the most fundamental traits of Biblically based leadership—attitude.

"Our attitudes may not be the assets that make us great leaders, but without good ones we will never reach our full potentials," Maxwell writes. "Our attitudes are the 'and then some' that allows us the little extra edge over those whose thinking is wrong."

Everyone knows that it's wrong to have a bad attitude. We learn that from our mothers. But Maxwell picks up where our mothers left off and forces us to deal with the bottom line realities of attitudes—good and bad. Then, in pure Maxwell form, he concludes with an action plan that allows us to change behaviors that deviate from the Biblical standard.

12

The Extra Plus in Leadership: Attitude

from *Developing the Leader Within You* by John Maxwell

When I speak at a leadership conference I often ask everyone to do this exercise:

Write the name of a friend whom you greatly admire.

_____

Write one thing that you most admire about that friend.

_____

I'd like you to take a moment and contemplate this exercise before you continue reading. I think you'll gain an interesting and important insight. The odds are high that the thing you most admire about your friend has to do with attitude. After all the conference participants have completed this exercise, I ask them to tell me their answers. I list the first twenty-five responses on an overhead projector for everyone to see. I put an *A* beside the characteristics that describe attitudes, an *S* beside those describing skills, and an *L* if the words deal with looks. Every time I conduct this exercise, 95 percent of the descriptive words represent attitudes for which the friends are admired.

Chuck Swindoll said, "The longer I live, the more I realize the impact of attitude on life. Attitude, to me, is more important than facts. It is more important than the past, than education, than money, than circumstances, than failures, than successes, than what other people think or say or do. It is more important than appearance, giftedness, or a skill. It will make or break a company, a church, or a home. The remarkable thing is that we have a choice every day regarding the attitude we will embrace for that day. We cannot change our past. Nor can we change the fact that people will act in a certain way. We also cannot change the inevitable. The only thing that we can do is play on the one string we have, and that is our attitude. I am convinced that life is 10 percent what happens to me and 90 percent how I react to it. And so it is with you—we are in charge of our attitudes.

Just as our attitudes are the extra pluses in life, they also make the difference in leading others. Leadership has less to do with position than it does with disposition. The disposition of a leader is important because it will influence the way the followers think and feel. Great leaders understand that the right attitude will set the right atmosphere that enables the right responses from others.

OUR ATTITUDES ARE OUR MOST IMPORTANT ASSETS.

Our attitudes may not be the assets that make us great leaders, but without good ones we will never reach our full potentials. Our attitudes are the "and then some" that allows us the little extra edge over those whose thinking is wrong. Walt Emerson said, "What lies behind us and what lies before us are tiny matters compared to what lies within us."

The 1983 Cos Report on American Business said that 94 percent of all Fortune 500 executives attributed their success more to attitude than to any other basic ingredient.

Robert Half International, a San Francisco consulting firm, recently asked vice-presidents and personnel directors at one hundred of America's largest companies to name the single greatest reason for firing an employee. The responses are very interesting and underscore the importance of attitude in the business world:

- Incompetence: 30 percent.
- Inability to get along with other workers: 17 percent.
- Dishonesty or lying: 12 percent.
- Negative attitude: 10 percent.

- Lack of motivation: 7 percent.
- Failure or refusal to follow instructions: 7 percent
- All other reasons: 8 percent.

Notice that although incompetence ranked first on the list, the next five were all attitude problems.

The Carnegie Institute not long ago analyzed the records of ten thousand persons and concluded that 15 percent of success is due to technical training. The other 85 percent is due to personality, and the primary personality trait identified by the research is attitude.

Our attitudes determine what we see and how we handle our feelings. These two factors greatly determine our success.

What we see: Psychology 101 taught me that we see what we are prepared to see. A suburbanite, unable to find his best saw, suspected his neighbor's son, who was always tinkering around with woodworking, had stolen it. During the next week everything the teenager did looked suspicious—the way he walked, the tone of his voice, his gestures. But when the older man found the saw behind his own workbench, where he had accidentally knocked it, he could no longer see anything at all suspicious in his neighbor's son. Flip Wilson taught me that what you see is what you get.

Nell Mohney, in her book *Beliefs Can Influence Attitudes*, pointedly illustrates this truth. Mohney tells of a double-blind experiment conducted in the San Francisco Bay area. The principal of a school called three professors together and said, "Because you three teachers are the finest in the system and you have the greatest expertise, we're going to give you ninety high-IQ students. We're going to let you move these students through this next year at their own pace and see how much they can learn."

Everyone was delighted—faculty and students alike.

Over the next year the professors and the students thoroughly enjoyed themselves. The professors were teaching the brightest students; the students were benefitting from the close attention and instruction of highly skilled teachers. By the end of the experiment, the students had achieved 20 to 30 percent more than the other students in the whole area.

The principal called the teachers in and told them, "I have a confession to make. I have to confess that you did not have ninety of the most intellectually prominent students. They were run of-the-mill students. We took ninety students at random from the system and gave them to you."

The teachers said, "This means that we are exceptional teachers."

The principal continued, "I have another confession. You're not the brightest of the teachers. Your names were the first three names drawn out of a hat."

The teachers asked, "What made the difference? Why did ninety students perform at such an exceptional level for a whole year?"

The difference, of course, was the teachers' expectations. Our expectations have a great deal to do with our attitudes. And these expectations may be totally false, but they will determine our attitudes.

How we handle our feelings: Notice I did not say our attitudes determine how we feel. There is a great difference between how we feel and how we handle our feelings. Everyone has times when they feel bad. Our attitudes cannot stop our feelings, but they can keep our feelings from stopping us. Unfortunately too many allow their feelings to control them until they end up like poor Ziggy in the comic strip.

He is sitting beneath a tree, gazing at the moon, and says, "I've been here and I've been there. I've been up and I've been down. I've been in and I've been out. I've been around and I've been about. But not once, not even once, have I ever been 'where it's at'!"

Every day I see people who are feeling controlled. A recent survey indicates that people with emotional problems are 144 percent more likely to have automobile accidents than those who are emotionally stable. An alarming factor revealed by this study is that one out of every five victims of fatal accidents had a quarrel within six hours before his or her accident.

Life is 10 percent what happens to me and 90 percent how I react to it.

Leadership has less to do with position than it does disposition.

We cannot continue to function in a manner that we do not truly believe about ourselves.

A leader's attitude is caught by his or her followers more quickly than his or her actions.

IT IS IMPROBABLE THAT A PERSON WITH A BAD ATTITUDE CAN CONTINUOUSLY BE A SUCCESS.

Norman Vincent Peale relates this story in his book, *Power of the Plus Factor*: "Once walking through the twisted little streets of Kowloon in Hong Kong, I came upon a tattoo studio. In the window were displayed samples of the tattoos available. On the chest or arms you could have tattooed an anchor or flag or mermaid or whatever. But what struck me with force were three words that could be tattooed on one's flesh, *Born to lose.*

"I entered the shop in astonishment and, pointing to those words, asked the Chinese tattoo artist, 'Does anyone really have that terrible phrase, *Born to lose*, tattooed on his body?'

"He replied, 'Yes, sometimes.'

"'But' I said, 'I just can't believe that anyone in his right mind would do that.'

"The Chinese man simply tapped his forehead and in broken English said, 'Before tattoo on body, tattoo on mind.'"

Once our minds are "tattooed" with negative thinking, our chances for long-term success diminish. We cannot continue to function in a manner that we do not truly believe about ourselves. Often I see people sabotage themselves because of wrong thinking.

What is the difference between a golfer who wins one golf tournament and an Arnold Palmer? Is it ability? Lucky breaks? Absolutely not! Where an average of less than two strokes per tournament separates the top twenty-five golfers in the world, the difference has to be something more than ability.

It's the attitude that makes the difference. People with negative thinking may start well, have a few good days, and win a match. But sooner or later (it's usually sooner), their attitudes will pull them down.

WE ARE RESPONSIBLE FOR OUR ATTITUDES.

Our destinies in life will never be determined by our complaining spirits or high expectations. Life is full of surprises and the adjustment of our attitudes is a life-long project.

The pessimist complains about the wind.

The optimist expects it to change.

The leader adjusts the sails.

My father, Melvin Maxwell, has always been my hero. He is a leader's leader. One of his strengths is his positive attitude. Recently Dad and Mom spent some time with my family. As he opened his briefcase, I noticed a couple of motivational attitude books.

I said, "Dad, you're seventy years old. You've always had a great attitude. Are you still reading that stuff?"

He looked me in the eye and said, "Son, I have to keep working on my thought life. I am responsible to have a great attitude and to maintain it. My attitude does not run on automatic."

Wow! That's a lesson for all of us. We choose what attitudes we have right now. And it's a continuing choice. I am amazed at the large number of adults who fail to take responsibility for their attitudes. When grumpy and someone asks why, they'll say, "I got up on the wrong side of the bed." When failure begins to plague their lives, they'll say, "I was born on the wrong side of the tracks." When life begins to flatten out and others in the family are still climbing, they'll say, "Well, I was in the wrong birth order in my family." When their marriages fail, they believe they married the wrong person. When someone else gets a promotion they wanted, it's because they were in the wrong place at the wrong time.

Do you notice something? They are blaming everyone else for their problems.

The greatest day in your life and mine is when we take total responsibility for our attitudes. That's the day we truly grow up.

An advisor to President Lincoln suggested a certain candidate for the Lincoln cabinet. But Lincoln refused, saying, "I don't like the man's face."

"But sir, he can't be responsible for his face," insisted the advisor.

"Every man over forty is responsible for his face," replied Lincoln, and the subject was dropped. No matter what you think about your attitude, it shows on your face!

The other day I saw a bumper sticker that read, "Misery is an option." I believe it! So does the daughter of a woman I heard about."

The woman and her daughter went Christmas shopping together. The crowds were awful. The woman had to skip lunch because she was on a tight schedule. She became tired and hungry, and her feet were hurting. She was more than a little irritable.

As they left the last store, she asked her daughter, "Did you see the nasty look that salesman gave me?" The daughter answered, "He didn't give it to you, Mom. You had it when you went in."

We cannot choose how many years we
   will live, but we can choose how much
   life those years will have.
We cannot control the beauty of our face,
   but we can control the expression on it.

We cannot control life's difficult moments, but we can choose to make life less difficult.

We cannot control the negative atmosphere of the world, but we can control the atmosphere of our minds.

Too often, we try to choose and control things we cannot.

Too, seldom, we choose to control what we can . . . our attitude.

IT'S NOT WHAT HAPPENS TO ME THAT MATTERS BUT WHAT HAPPENS IN ME.

Hugh Downs says that a happy person is not a person with a certain set of circumstances, but rather a person with a certain set of attitudes. Too many people believe that happiness is a condition. When things are going great, they're happy. When things are going bad, they're sad. Some people have what I call "destination disease." They think that happiness can be found in a position or a place. Others have what I call "someone sickness." They think happiness results from knowing or being with a particular person.

I am impressed with the philosophy of the following statement: "God chooses what we go through. We choose how we go through it." It describes Viktor Frankl's attitude. He was terribly mistreated in a Nazi concentration camp. His words to his persecutors have been an inspiration to millions of people. He said, "The one thing you cannot take away from me is the way

I choose to respond to what you do to me. The last of one's freedoms is to choose one's attitude in any given circumstance."

Clara Barton, the founder of the American Red Cross, understood the importance of choosing a right attitude even in wrong situations. She was never known to hold a grudge against anyone. One time a friend recalled to her a cruel thing that had happened to her some years previously, but Clara seemed not to remember the incident.

"Don't you remember the wrong that was done to you?" the friend asked.

"No," Clara answered calmly. "I distinctly remember forgetting that."

Many times people who have suffered adverse situations in their lives become bitter and angry. Over time, their lives will be negative and hardened toward others. The tendency for them is to point back to a difficult time and say, "That incident ruined my life." What they do not realize is that the incident called for an attitude decision—a response. Their wrong attitude choice, not the condition, ruined their lives.

C. S. Lewis said, "Everytime you make a choice you are turning the control part of you, the part that chooses, into something a little different from what it was before. And taking your life as a whole, with all your innumerable choices, you are slowly turning this control thing into either a heavenly creature or into a hellish one."

THE LEADER'S ATTITUDE HELPS DETERMINE THE ATTITUDES OF THE FOLLOWERS.

Leadership is influence. People catch our attitudes just like they catch our colds—by getting close to us. One of the most gripping thoughts to ever enter my mind centers on my influence as a leader. It is important that I possess a great attitude, not only for my own success, but also for the benefit of others. My responsibilities as a leader must always be viewed in light of the many, not just myself.

Dr. Frank Crane reminds us that a ball rebounds from the wall with precisely the force with which it was thrown against the wall. There is a law in physics to the effect that action is equal to reaction. That law is also true in the realm of influence. In fact its effects multiply with a leader's influence. The action of a leader multiplies in reaction because there are several followers. To a smile given, many smiles return. Anger unleashed toward others results in much anger returned from many.

There are few actual victims of fate. The generous are helped and the stingy are shunned.

Remember the four-minute mile? People had been trying to achieve it since the days of the ancient Greeks. In fact folklore has it that the Greeks had lions chase the runners, thinking that would make them run faster. They also tried

drinking tiger's milk—not the stuff you get down at the health food store, but the real thing. Nothing they tried worked. So they decided it was impossible for a person to run a mile in four minutes or less. And for over a thousand years everyone believed it. Our bone structure is all wrong. Wind resistance is too great. We have inadequate lung power. There were a million reasons.

Then one man, one single human being, proved that the doctors, the trainers, the athletes, and the millions of runners before him, who tried and failed, were all wrong. And, miracle of miracles, the year after Roger Bannister broke the four-minute mile, thirty-seven other runners broke the four-minute mile. The year after that three hundred runners broke the four-minute mile. And a few years ago in a single race in New York, thirteen out of thirteen runners broke the four-minute mile. In other words, a few decades ago the runner who finished dead last in the New York race would have been regarded as having accomplished the impossible.

What happened? There were no great breakthroughs in training. No one discovered how to control wind resistance. Human bone structure and physiology didn't suddenly improve. But human attitudes did.

You can accomplish your goals, if you set them. Who says you're not tougher, smarter, better, harder-working, more able than your competition? It does not matter if they say you can't do it. What matters, the only thing that matters, is if you say it.

Until Roger Bannister came along, we all believed the experts. And so, "the experts" continue to keep others from reaching their potential. Why? Because experts have influence. In fact I believe that a leader's attitude is caught by his followers more quickly than his actions. An attitude is reflected by others even when they don't follow the action. An attitude can be expressed without a word being spoken.

The effect of a leader's attitude on others is the main reason for the importance of considering a candidate's attitude when hiring executives.

Practicing psychologists list five areas needing significant appraisal when employees are being considered for executive promotion: ambition; attitudes toward policy; attitudes toward colleagues; supervisory skills; and attitudes toward excessive demands on time and energy. A candidate who is out of balance in one or more of these areas would be likely to project a negative attitude and, therefore, prove to be a poor leader.

Take a moment and list the negative attitudes you possess that are influencing others right now.

1.

2.

3.

4.

HOW TO CHANGE YOUR ATTITUDE

Many people seem to suffer from what Ashley Montagu the great Rutgers anthropologist, called *psychosclerosis*. Psychosclerosis is like arteriosclerosis, which is hardening of the arteries. Psychosclerosis is hardening of the attitudes.

David Neiswanger of the Menninger Foundation says that if each of us can be helped by science to live a hundred years, what will it profit us if our hates and fears, our loneliness and our remorse, will not permit us to enjoy them?

The following sections will help you to help yourself in changing your attitude.

Review.

Several years ago my wife, Margaret, and I bought our first house. Our limited finances forced us to find some ways of getting what we wanted without spending a great deal of money. We agreed we would work on the front yard ourselves to save labor expenses and still create a proper setting for our home. It looked great.

One day, while I was standing in our backyard, I began to realize that we had spent no time or money making the back look good. Why? Because it couldn't be seen by others as they passed our house. We were careless about the area that was hidden.

That is exactly what people do in their personal lives. Their appearances, which can be seen outwardly, are spared no expense or energy. Yet their attitudes are neglected and underdeveloped. Remember the opening part of this chapter? Go back and read it again, and then put the necessary energy and effort into changing the inner areas of your life.

The Six Stages of Attitude Change

1. *Identify problem feelings*. This is the earliest stage of awareness and the easiest to declare.

2. *Identify problem behavior*. Now we go beneath the surface. What triggers wrong feelings? Write down actions that result in negative feelings.

3. *Identify problem thinking*. William James said, "That which holds our attention determines our action."

4. *Identify right thinking*. Write on paper the thinking that is right and what you desire. Because your feelings come from your thoughts, you can control your feelings by changing one thing—your thoughts!

5. *Make a public commitment to right thinking*. Public commitment becomes powerful commitment.

6. *Develop a plan for right thinking*. This plan should include:

- A written definition of desired right thinking
- A way to measure progress
- A daily measuring of progress
- A person to whom you are accountable

- A daily diet of self-help materials
- Associating with right thinking people

This is a general plan for attitude self-improvement. The other steps will increase the probability of your success.

Resolve.

Whenever a leader needs to ask others to make a commitment of time, two questions must always be answered: "Can they?" (this deals with ability) and "Will they?" (this deals with attitude). The more important question of the two is "Will they?" Two other questions usually answer the "Will they?" issue. The first is, "Is the timing right?" In other words, are the conditions right to enable positive change? The second question is, "Is their temperature hot?" Are right conditions accompanied with a red hot desire to pay the price necessary for needed change? When both questions can be answered with a resounding Yes! then the resolve is strong and success is possible.

Reframe.

Dennis Waitley says that the winners in life think constantly in terms of I can, I will, and I am. Losers, on the other hand, concentrate their waking thoughts on what they should have done or what they didn't do. If we don't like our performances, then we must first change the picture.

Cancer researchers at King's College in London did a long-term study of fifty-seven breast cancer victims who'd had mastectomies. They found that seven out of ten women "with a fighting spirit" were alive ten years later, while four out of five women "who felt hopeless" at the diagnosis had died.

The study of hope as it affects health even has a fancy name—*psychoneuroimmunology.* Harborview Medical Center in Seattle is researching in this field, and their findings support the conclusions of the King's College researchers. In a two-year study of burn victims, the Harborview research team discovered that patients with positive attitudes recovered more quickly than those with negative ones.

Reframing your attitude means:

I may not be able to change the world I
see around me, but I can change the way
I see the world within me.

Re-enter

As you begin changing your thinking, start immediately to change your behavior. Begin to act the part of the person you would like to become. Take action on the behavior you admire by making it your behavior. Too many people want to feel, then take action. This never works.

One day while visiting a doctor's office, I read this in a medical magazine: "We hear it almost every day . . . sigh . . . sigh . . . sigh. 'I just can't get myself moti-vated to lose weight, test my blood sugar, etc.' And we hear an equal number of sighs from diabetes educators who can't get their patients motivated to do the right things for their diabetes and health.

"We have news for you. Motivation is not going to strike you like lightning. And motivation is not something that someone else—nurse, doctor, family member—can bestow or force on you. The whole idea of motivation is a trap. Forget motivation. Just do it. Exercise, lose weight, test your blood sugar, or whatever. Do it without motivation. And then, guess what? After you start doing the thing, that's when the motivation comes and makes it easy for you to keep on doing it.

"Motivation," says John Bruner, "is like love and happiness. It's a by-product. When you're actively engaged in doing something, the motivation to keep on doing it sneaks up and zaps you when you least expect it."

As Harvard psychologist Jerome Brunet says, "You're more likely to act yourself into feeling than feel yourself into action. So act! Whatever it is you know you should do, do it."

The attitude development of our children, Elizabeth and Joel Porter, is very important to my wife, Margaret, and me. We learned a long time ago that the most effective way to change our children's attitudes is to work on their behaviors. But when we tell one of our children, "Change your attitude," the message is too general and the change we want is unclear. A more effective approach is explaining behaviors that signify bad attitudes. If we help them change their behaviors, the attitudes will change on their own. Instead of saying to our kids, "Get a grateful attitude," we ask them to give one compliment to every member of the family each day. As this becomes a habit in their lives, the attitude of gratitude follows.

Repeat.

Paul Myer said, "Attitudes are nothing more than habits of thought, and habits can be acquired. An action repeated becomes an attitude realized." Once, while leading a conference, I was asked for a simple plan to help a person change some wrong attitudes. I recommended two things to help her change her attitude. First:

> Say the right words,
> Read the right books,
> Listen to the right tapes,
> Be with the right people,
> Do the right things,
> Pray the right prayer.

The second was to do number one every day, not just once or only when you feel like it, and watch your life change for the better.

Renewal.

Fortunately over a period of time a positive attitude can replace a negative one. Again, let me emphasize that the battle is never over, but it is well worth our efforts. The more that negative thoughts are weeded out and replaced by positive ones, the more personal renewal will be experienced. My friend Lena Walker wrote a tribute about her grandfather and a practice in his life that he passed on to her. These words effectively describe the ongoing process of attitude development and the worthiness of overcoming negative thinking.

Each year as spring approaches, my thoughts turn to a white-haired old man who went forth at this time of year to do battle. The enemy was not flesh and blood, but a small yellow flower called "mustard." As one gazes out over the fields and meadows, this yellow touch seems harmless enough, but year-by-year it continues its march, and can eventually take over entire fields. Each spring my grandfather would walk through his fields pulling these yellow flowers out by the roots.

Eventually I was married and lived on a farm in Ohio. Each spring I, too, would look out and see these same yellow flowers. The first few years on the farm I did nothing about them, but as maturity came upon me, I could see the wisdom of my grandfather's efforts. I, too, decided to go forth as he had done and do battle with the enemy.

Now, each year as I walk through the fields pulling an occasional mustard plant, I feel I am doing it in tribute to my grandfather.

To me this weed represents our bad habits and negative thoughts. We need to constantly prune out these things so our lives can be lush and green in our quest for a happy and productive life.

PART FIVE
The Future

Bob Buford will never forget the day he walked alone across a limestone bluff some 200 feet above the waters of the Rio Grande River. On a lark, his 24-year-old son and two friends had attempted to swim across the river, and Buford was facing the reality that the river had taken his son's life.

"Here's something you can't dream your way out of," Buford told himself. "Here's something you can't think your way out of, buy your way out of, or work your way out of. . . . This is something you can only trust your way out of."

By taking an eternal perspective and focusing on the inspiration of the all-too-short life his son had lived, Buford continued a journey that has seen him rise from being a leader of a company to being a leader in a movement.

Through such organizations as The Leadership Network, FaithWorks, and The Foundation, Buford is having a dramatic impact as an influencer in the movement of connecting faith and work. *Halftime,* published in 1994, is his life message, but it's also a brand in and of itself. In it, Buford brings raw intelligence and rich life experiences together with a vibrant heart for the person of Jesus Christ.

When Buford found himself at a turning point in his life, he did some serious life analysis and reached the conclusion that the first half of his life had focused on success rather than significance. His search would lead to a message—how to move from success to significance—that is feeding a starved generation of Baby Boomers.

For some, the answer is to leave the success-oriented job for a significance-oriented job. For others, however, it's a process. This chapter from *Halftime* focuses on how to stay in the game with an adjusted plan. In affect, Buford challenges midlifers to discover—or rediscover—their callings.

The bottom line: Periodic times of career evaluation that include the possibility of career adjustment contribute to work satisfaction, and more importantly, life impact.

Buford describes this as "optimum job fit," and he says it is not necessarily discovered by quitting your job. It is found by looking at the critical requirements of a job and overlapping that with who you are created to be.

"The key to a successful second half is not a change of jobs," he writes, "it is a change of heart." With a changed heart, you can determine if you need to change careers, stay in your current position or live out some combination of the two. You can discover how your skills fit within God's divine calling, and that will lead to significance in your second half.

13 Staying in the Game, but Adjusting the Plan

from *Halftime* by Bob Buford

MY SECOND HALF began when I walked away from my full-time, hands-on involvement with work. You probably cannot do that. But even if you can't, you can still have a second half.

By the time you get into halftime, your attitude toward your job may range from "I love my job so much I'd do it even if they didn't pay me" to "I can't stand what I do no matter how much money I make." I was lucky enough to be pretty close to the first response, but I realize there are many who are closer to the second. In fact, my hunch is that quite a few people do not like their job very much, and use it mainly as a means to an end.

I recall a young man who was a cold call, straight commission salesperson. He was one of those guys who didn't make a penny if he didn't sell something. No base salary. No drawing a salary on his commission. Just knock on doors and try to sell, and in this case, he sold fairly low-ticket items: notions and knickknacks to general stores, and hardware stores.

But this guy was good: He sold enough to earn a six-figure income. That's a ton of knickknacks! Like most salesmen, he had a lot of drive and a lot of enthusiasm. In fact, he was so enthusiastic that I remarked about how much he must love selling. "I hate it," he replied. "But I love the pay." I mused to myself, recalling how my son, Ross, used to say, "I want to live to work, not work to live."

For me, my career demanded just those things I enjoyed giving, and it rewarded me with a great deal of satisfaction and with not a little money. To me, there was nothing more exhilarating than putting together a deal, negotiating the details, then celebrating after the handshake. I loved to develop a strategy to make the deal work. I was successful and received plenty of strokes, so it was not easy for me to decide to hand over the day-to-day operation of my business to a team of other people. In a sense, I was depriving myself of the pleasure I derived from my job.

Some people think that their problems would be over if they could just walk away from their job. In fact, this is one of the reasons why so many people stay in the first half: They get tired of the rat race and, instead of planning a successful midlife crisis, they jump ship. Change jobs. Start a business. Go independent.

None of the above are bad options, but I plead with you: Beware the urge to "get away from it all." That is not what the second half is all about. I know people who are well into their second halves who are still working at the same job they started with and who will be there to get the gold watch. The key to a successful second half is not a change of jobs; it is a change of heart, a change in the way you view the world and order your life. That might involve a completely new career or holding on to your present position. Usually, it is something between the two.

SEISMIC TESTING

Being from Texas, I can't help but have learned a few things about the oil business. I'm far from being an expert, mind you, but one of the things I have learned is that you don't just go out and pick a spot and start drilling. If you want to minimize your risks, you do some seismic testing—which is basically a sophisticated way to check out the landscape to see what it might produce. Since the size and shape of a subsurface formation is unknown, an electronic device is used to shoot sonar-like impulses down toward the formation from different points of view. The matter starts to take shape as it is seen from the various perspectives.

In terms of second-half seismic testing, your "subsurface formation" is that imponderable matter regarding how you will restructure your life. Your idea is indistinct in size and shape, and you can only see it from a limited viewpoint, so you go to six or eight different people you trust and ask them how they see it. Their "sonar" will reflect a part of the picture that you could not see before, and eventually the most vague and inchoate matters will begin to assume a definite size and shape. Then at least you know whether to drill or not.

You may think that once I decided what was in the box, I quickly handed the reins of my business over to a subordinate and walked out the door looking for new, albeit tamer, dragons to slay. Believe me, that would have been a big mistake, even though I was financially set for life and could afford some false starts. Instead, I did some seismic testing. I knew that I was gifted in the area of human organizations, and I also knew I enjoyed working in that area immensely. I could have stayed on in the human organization I had built, for I was assured continued success there, but I had already tasted success; it was significance I was after—something that got closer to both who I was and what was in the box. I did not see my cable television business as a primary source of significance in my life.

Neither did my adviser, Mike Kami. His advice was simple, and I wasn't quite ready for it: "Sell your company and invest the money in the ministry-oriented projects you've been talking about."

I sat there, stunned by the implications of this decision. Linda appeared no less stunned. I could almost see the stereotypical images of ministers, missionaries, and monastics passing through her mind. Would we be a philanthropic couple passing out money until our sack was empty? Would we be required to dress like a minister and his spouse? Had life as we'd known and enjoyed it come to a sudden, crashing, newly impoverished end?

Fortunately, I did some seismic testing. I sought the advice of two Christian leaders: Ray Steadman, then pastor of a church in Palo Alto, California, and James Dobson, popular author and founder of Focus on the Family. In their own way, each warned me: "If you sell your company, you will lose your platform and no one will return your calls." It was clear that I needed to be far more certain about where I was going with my life before I made any big plans.

So I called together a group of trusted advisers that included Fred Smith Sr., Paul Robbins, and Harold Myra of *Christianity Today*. Together, they had a broad overview and deep knowledge of the area in which I was preparing to work: the body of Christ in the United States. They knew how much I enjoyed working on organizational schemes, and that I wanted to spend a good share of my time on kingdom work. I asked them, "What

are the opportunities for someone with my particular design?"

They reminded me of a new breed of churches that was very large and attempting to do church differently. "Maybe you could help them somehow," they suggested. So I invited a group of pastors together, asked Paul to serve as a nondirective moderator to ask them some questions, then sat back and listened.

Listening is a big part of seismic testing; it helps you discover areas of usefulness. I learned what these pastors perceived would be useful to them, and then continued my testing by facilitating focus groups of senior pastors from large churches. Eventually these pastors narrowed down their discussions to three things they felt would be useful to them, and I saw my second-half calling take shape.

As a direct result of this kind of testing, I was able to develop a network and support system that serves a unique group of people in Christian ministry. There is nothing magic about pastors of large churches; it just happens that, in God's providence, my interest in human organizations matched up nicely with their need to understand the dynamics of what is happening with their churches. If I was wired differently, I could have been hooked up just as easily with executives of overseas missions agencies or a network of small, rural churches. But had I rushed out of my session with Mike Kami and jumped at the first church-type job available, I probably would not have found something so closely aligned to who I am.

There are two keys to successful seismic testing. The first is to know who you are, and the second is to seek out reliable counsel. When I sought guidance from two friends, I asked, "What can I do to be useful?" They responded, "What does the 'I' consist of?" That's a very important question for anyone looking into the second half, because you cannot operate out of a strength that God doesn't give you.

Suppose you have often felt guilty about not doing enough evangelizing, so, when your second half rolls around, you decide to quit your job to become a preacher or a missionary. Instead, it might be much better to begin this decision-making process with a full knowledge and acceptance of who you are. Honestly assess your gifts and abilities. Is evangelism your gift? If it is something you enjoy doing and can do well—then do some seismic testing before you sign up for seminary or head to Africa. Assist your pastor on some calls to people interested in learning about Jesus or volunteer for a short-term missions assignment. If these brief explorations come back positive, then get more serious about what to do. If they come back negative, you will have saved yourself a lot of trouble.

What you do best for God will rise out of that core being he has created within you. Do you remember our Lord's parable

of the talents? The wonderful message from this story is that you and I will only be held accountable for what we were given, not for what others might have or expect from us. The guy who was given only two talents and doubled them was esteemed as highly as the guy who started out with five. We are not all given the same equipment, but we are expected to know what we were given and find ways to invest ourselves wisely.

LOW-COST PROBES

I have a friend almost exactly my age who had come to a point similar to my own at halftime. He decided that God was the central, motivating factor in his life and that he wanted to find some way of giving his gift of leadership back to God. At about the same time, he was offered the CEO spot in a two-billion-dollar, highly leveraged company with operations ranging as far west as Thailand and as far east as Europe. It would be a tough, demanding, and challenging job with plenty of prestige and an annual salary approaching a million dollars. It was the type of position that people in the business community would die for . . . in fact, many do.

But if he took the job, he would be committed to at least five years—time that he had hoped to be spending in kingdom work.

He had also been thinking about going

to seminary, so he came to me with these two choices: Fortune 500 or Hermeneutics 101. He had already made the decision to put God in the box, but he did not know whether that meant full-time, professional Christian ministry or something else.

I told him to take the CEO spot, forget about seminary, and to engage in some low-cost probes. To me, he had no choice. If he went to seminary, he would emerge three years later as a rank amateur at over fifty years of age. He might land an associate minister's job at a larger church and, by the time he was fifty-five, get a senior position at a church struggling to keep its head above water. Did my friend really think God gave him twenty-five years of training in business management and executive leadership so that he could pastor a medium-sized church struggling to find itself?

That did not mean, however, that my friend needed to disavow his allegiance to God. Low-cost probes involve practical explorations in the field or fields in which you think you would like to spend your second half. My friend, for example, may need to stay in the midst of international business, but look into starting an informal network of Bible studies for other CEOs. It would take some phone calls, a few faxes, and a couple of trial balloons to show him if that is really a need, and if he's the one to fill it. Or, if he senses the need to eventually leave his career and work more in professional ministry, he

might consider doing some consulting for Christian organizations—pro bono, if necessary.

My inviting a group of pastors to a meeting is another example of a low-cost probe. I had done my seismic testing by seeking out the counsel of trusted advisers who pointed me in the right direction, but I did not jump in with both feet. If that first meeting of pastors had fallen flat, my investment of time and money was such that I could have easily tried something else.

The point of low-cost probes is to gain some hands-on experience in combining your gifts with service to God and the church. It's done in business all the time in the form of market research, product testing, pilot projects and the like. The reason people don't do it individually as they approach the second half is that they're still doings things the first-half way: full speed ahead with both feet. Remember, this second-half decision is about something more important than just another investment, just another sale. Slow down. Be deliberate. Test the waters.

THE HALF-SPEED OPTION

Let's say you really like your job and, frankly, you feel you need it. You need the security of a regular paycheck, health insurance, and pension, and you also enjoy the identity it gives you. You like being sales manager for Midtown Associates. Can someone like you look forward to a rewarding second half?

Actually, many people will fit this description. And the group really grows when we add those who don't necessarily like their work, but who find that leaving is not an option.

The good news is that people in this group certainly can have a second half that's better than the first. Let's face it. By the time you've been at something for ten to twenty years, you've pretty well mastered it. You've learned to delegate, you have a network of people whom you know, you know the landscape, you've grown a productive list of clients, and you've found ways to get through each day without rushing at breakneck speed.

If you're really honest with yourself, you can probably work at half speed and still excel. That's what a lawyer friend of mine is doing. He is a senior partner in a very prestigious law firm who handles cases for some of the most powerful and famous people in the country. Scott (not his real name) loved what he was doing and was world-class at it, yet he sensed there was more to life than putting together megadeals—he sensed that he was missing something. There were second-half things he wanted to do, but he didn't want to walk away from a practice he'd worked so hard to build. Then he realized he could stay with his firm and

still have time to invest himself in a very worthy project involving the public school systems around his state. Now when you ask him what he does for a living, he responds, somewhat facetiously, "I'm trying to convince my law partners that I still practice law." What he's really doing is taking half the time it used to take to drive his career and putting it into this new second-half commitment.

Or consider another acquaintance who's a public school teacher. He's one of the best science teachers in his state and would just as soon retire "in the saddle," but he too has some second-half goals to pursue. One of these is to use his administrative skills to provide business leadership for his local church. He started out just like my lawyer friend: hard-charging, working sixteen-hour days, pushing the envelope in order to become top in his field. Both men love their work and do not feel it's time to leave it, so they are using the additional time and energy that comes from doing a good job at half speed to fulfill their second-half goals.

You see, when it comes to having a better second half than the first, it doesn't matter whether you're a millionaire CEO, a high-paid lawyer, or a teacher. What's important is that you start off by discovering the way God built you so that you can use your uniquely developed talents for him.

The man on the airplane was a veteran television executive who had, to say the least, a colorful personality. And when we asked him if he knew Bob Briner, the long-time president of ProServe Television, the man didn't answer with a simple, "yes."

It's hard to sprinkle a series of casual expletives into a one-word answer, so he expanded his response into a couple of paragraphs. And as he began to wind down, the man said that while he personally had never been very religious, he knew Briner to be an excellent businessman who also was really good at living out his faith in his professional life.

It was one of the grandest compliments the man could have given Briner. During a career as an influential force in the world of professional sports, television, and business, Briner intentionally, overtly, and skillfully melded the world of Scripture with the world of daily living.

Briner died in 1999 following a bout with cancer, but the importance of integrating the spiritual and the professional was his life message and his legacy. He shared that message passionately and persuasively in *Roaring Lambs*.

In this chapter, Briner explored the concept of being salt in the modern work world. Salt, Briner pointed out, retards spoilage, but it doesn't stop it. So it can't be put on the shelf and forgotten. It has to be used—in all areas of life.

Briner's particular passion was for the arts, the media, and academia—areas that have an obvious impact on society. Why, Briner wondered, do we make such a big deal of preparing people for careers as missionaries to foreign countries and such a small deal about people preparing for careers in the mainstream work world—especially those careers that so clearly lack and need Christ?

Briner points out that our mandate to be salt and light might mean working in professions that are shunned by most followers of Jesus.

Briner's legacy is a challenging message that will shake followers of Christ out of the saltshaker of the church and into the meat of the world.

14

Salt: Make Use of It

from *Roaring Lambs* by Bob Briner

I HAVE A friend who raises sheep. He says they're among the most misunderstood of farm animals. True, he says, they are meek. They need someone to follow, and if they don't have a thoughtful, caring shepherd, they generally get themselves into trouble. Bigtime trouble.

But, says my friend the sheep farmer, their trust in their shepherd is so strong that they will do anything to follow the guy. In fact, he says, they can be the bravest, most assertive creatures when they feel secure in the care of their shepherd.

That's the kind of lambs we ought to be. We have a Shepherd we can trust fully, so we really ought to be out there on the front lines of battle for the cause of the Gospel. The fact that we aren't has a lot to do with our understanding (or misunderstanding) of those oft-quoted words from Matthew 5:13: *You are the salt.*

To the average Christian, salt is something that comes in a blue box and hides on the shelf until it's needed. That's our first mistake, but don't be too hard on yourself. If you have spent more than twenty minutes in church, you have probably heard that you are the salt of the earth. And most of what you've heard has probably made you feel guilty about not doing enough stuff. Never mind the fact that if you were gifted as an artist, businessman, or civic leader, no one could quite tell you what stuff you ought to be doing. All you had to look up to were people "in ministry" who were "called" to full-time Christian service. You really want to be salt? Take an early retirement and go to Haiti as a missionary.

That's not necessarily being salt, if I may mix a metaphor, nor is it what's required to be a roaring lamb.

This "salt" Scripture is so familiar, so much a part of the evangelical vernacular that it has lost much of its power. It is heard so often and used so much even in everyday language that its imperative has dissipated.

I don't know about you, but when I think of someone who exemplifies this verse, I think of a little old lady who's been a great prayer warrior or an older, congenial gentleman who has given a lot to the church. Nothing against little old ladies and kind elderly men, but I've never been able to relate to that kind of person.

Maybe someday I'll be one of those grandfatherly old men who sits close to the front every Sunday morning at church, but in the meantime I've got a business to run. Can I be salt also? Can I sit across the table from the chairman of the Sony Corporation and still have an impact on the world for Jesus? To most people in twentieth-century America, someone who is "the salt of the earth" is someone who is a rather dull, plodding, conforming individual—a hard worker, maybe, and honest but pretty tame, a loyal churchman who seldom does anything outside of church.

However, the salt Jesus has in mind is stinging, biting, cleansing, and presenting and is anything but dull, anything but tame. To be the kind of salt Christ spoke about is to be on the cutting edge, in the fray, at the forefront of battle.

When Jesus said, "You are the salt of the earth," He was speaking to anyone then or now who accepts Him as Savior. It is one of the clearest declarations in Scripture from Jesus to His followers. Notice, He did not say for us to become salt. He said we are salt. Once we accept Him into our lives we automatically are the salt of the earth.

The second part of the verse gives us insight into what being salt should mean: "But if the salt loses its saltiness, how can it be made salty again? It is no longer good for anything, except to be thrown out and trampled by men." So, just being

salt is not enough. In fact, if we are salt and are not being salty, isn't it fair to say that we are good-for-nothing Christians? That's what the Scripture says to me.

But the question is what do we *do*? How do we act as salt in our world? The answer lies in the way salt is used. Salt is both a seasoning and a preservative. It seasons by adding taste and enhancing flavor. It preserves by cleansing and retarding spoilage. In both cases, the salt must be brought in contact with is object for its power to be realized. Sitting in the shaker, it does no good. It might just as well be thrown out.

More than twenty years ago Stanley Jones, the great Methodist writer and missionary, was asked to name the number-one problem in the church. His quick reply was "Irrelevance." Not that the church was inherently irrelevant, but that Christians were failing to show in concrete ways and to tell in cogent understandable terms how the person of Christ is relevant to all of life in the twentieth century. Elton Trueblood, the influential Quaker teacher and writer, puts it another way. He says, "It is hard to exaggerate the degree to which the modern church seems irrelevant to modern man."

The number one way, then, for Christians to be the salt Christ commands them to be is to teach His relevance, to demonstrate His relevance, to live His relevance in every area of life. We cannot accomplish this by talking only to ourselves, writing only for ourselves, associating only with ourselves and working only in the "safe" careers and professions. Being salt is not nearly so much about having more pastors and missionaries as it is about having many more committed Christian lay people thinking strategically about and acting on ways to build the kingdom in such areas as public policy, advertising, media, higher education, entertainment, the arts, and sports.

Keeping Christ bottled up in the churches is keeping salt in the shakers, and He does not go where we do not take Him. We need to take Him everywhere and show His relevance and the relevance of His Word to every aspect of modern life. This is not an option, it is an imperative, a scriptural imperative.

The process of obeying Christ's command to be salt is about penetration, just as many of Christ's commands are about penetration. Salt must penetrate the meat to preserve it. Christians must penetrate key areas of culture to have a preserving effect. And penetration does not mean standing outside and lobbing hand grenades of criticism over the wall. It is not about being reactionary and negative. It is about being inside through competence and talent and, with God's help and the Holy Spirit's leading, offering scripturally-based alternatives to those things that are corrupting and evil.

We need to understand that real Christian penetration is not easy. For example,

it is infinitely easier to boycott objectionable television programs than it is to create, produce, sell, and distribute a quality television program or series that would extol virtue, family values, Christian courage, and eternal truths. Participating in a boycott of the products of companies sponsoring trashy television programs might make us feel good and righteous, but it has very little to do with being salt in the world. It certainly does not call for the kind of commitment Christ asks for. Compare sending a few dollars to the boycott headquarters and refraining from buying a certain brand of soap for a few weeks to committing oneself, one's resources, and one's career to providing for the homes of the nation television programming that would glorify Christ. The first is trivial, almost frivolous, the second worthy of prayerful support and sacrificial commitment. When, Christians criticize, carp, and complain but offer no alternatives, the world rolls its eyes, snickers, and moves on. It is really only when we offer a "more excellent way" that we command or deserve much attention.

Dr. Ray Pritchard, Bible scholar and the senior pastor of Calvary Memorial Church in Oak Park, Illinois, says, "Being the salt of the earth means acting as a purifying agent to hinder the spread of evil. We who follow Jesus Christ are to be a 'moral disinfectant' stopping the spread of evil. We are to be the conscience of the community, speaking out for what is true and right."

To do that, we must be in that community. We must be a part of that community. We cannot be much of a "moral disinfectant" from afar. It does very little good to commiserate with each other about how evil the "Hollywood community" is, or how godless the television community is, or how the print media seems to always take the low road, or how government policy makers seem to never consider biblical truths, or how corrupt the music and arts scenes are. Sitting in the pews wringing our hands about decay in the world is not being salt. Neither is decrying the evil without offering positive alternatives.

Certainly, there's much in this world that is alarming, but I believe there's a better way to do something about it than simply preach against it. The best way to stop the spread of evil is to replace it with something good.

The best way to stop the spread of popular music with its vulgar suggestive lyrics is to record great music that uplifts the human spirit. Christian artist Amy Grant retards the spread of evil every time one of her records plays on a secular radio station. Those who criticize her for "crossing over" into the secular world with music that is not distinctly Christian forget one thing. Her music takes up the air time that could have gone to one of the multitude of recordings offering only degradation and moral rot. Amy Grant is being salt in the world. She's high on my

list of candidates for a Roaring Lamb Hit of Fame. One Amy Grant hit record provides more salt for a decaying world than a thousand sermons decrying the evils of popular music or nationwide boycotts of recording companies. We need more Amy Grants much more than we need more reactionary sermons. We also need Christian musicians, talent managers, producers, and record-company executives to bring real salt to the whole influential popular music industry.

Don't get me wrong. There are times when following the call of God demands that we speak out loudly against flagrant evil. But if that's all we do, particularly if most of our speaking out is only to each other, we are not being salt. The way to be salt is to replace evil with good, not to just sound off against the evil.

The Genesis account of Sodom and Gomorrah is very instructive about the preserving power of righteous people and illustrates the way God's people bring the saving salt to every situation. As long as there were even a few righteous people within Sodom, God spared it. Even when Lot was the only righteous person within the city, it was preserved until he left. Today, Christians are called to occupy the lost provinces of society and hold on to "the last man" the way Lot did. We need to abandon the mentality that some professions are just too corrupt for Christians to enter. We are called to be the Lots of every legitimate area of human endeavor, preserving it from the wrath of God. The longer we preserve it and the longer we act as salt there, the more opportunity there will be for men and women to be won to the person of Christ. Being salt does not always mean we "evangelize," but by replacing evil with good, we enhance the climate for evangelism.

In the life of the Spirit, in the battle of good vs. evil, in the effort to preserve goodness, there are no effective salt substitutes. If Christians do not provide the salt, it's not there, and life loses much of its flavor, much of its meaningfulness. Consider the history of Christianity in Europe. Over the past twenty or so years, I have made more than a hundred visits to London. One year I spent more time in London than in any other city except my home city of Dallas. Using our apartment in Paris as a base, I have become very familiar with the great capital cities of Europe. Sadly, these cities and their societies are increasingly secular and humanistic to the point that they are almost pagan. The church may be physically present, but much of its spiritual vitality has been sapped and is, for all practical purposes, gone. And as dynamic, relevant Christianity has gone, so too has the life-enhancing taste of salt that Christians bring to life and living. Even in these glamorous tourist destinations, which everyone wants to visit, once you get past the intrigue and into the lives of the people you do not need to be particularly perceptive to notice the existential angst that seems to have everyone in its grip. There's no salt. Conspicuously absent is the sharpness and spice brought to a society by the penetrating salt of an active church.

Will the same thing happen here? Some say it's already happening. Because of our historic ties with Europe and Great Britain, these areas are, perhaps, the most revealing examples of what a society once mightily influenced by the message of Christ can become when it becomes almost totally secularized and the church survives primarily as an anachronism. Certainly there are dynamic Christians and wonderful churches in both Britain and Europe, but the numbers are now so small as to be demographically insignificant. To use Alfred North Whitehead's phrase about the church, "Its institutions no longer direct the patterns of life." It is irrelevant. There is no salt.

In America, with all our problems—the extreme secularization of society with its accompanying commitment to instant gratification—the church still provides a measure of salt for our society. Not enough, but it is still there, adding flavor to our lives. The trend, however, is toward the secular, the profane, the here and now. If we are content to let that continue, all we need to do is stay the course and keep preaching to each other as we watch a culture fade into oblivion. But if we want to see our society revitalized, we need to add some salt. We need to let the lambs roar.

I've spent a good deal of my professional career in two arenas: professional sports and television. I may be biased, but I don't think you could name two more influential fields. From highly visible athletes to a steady stream of programming into your homes, these two fields are truly culture shaping. And they illustrate both the best and the worst of Christian involvement in the world.

Certainly, anyone following big-time sports in America is well aware of its problems. Dishonesty, exploitation, drugs, illicit sex, ego gratification gone out of control, and the attempt to deify money are all very significant problems not only for professional sports but also for college sports and, in some communities, even high school sports. In his bestseller, *Friday Night Lights*, H. G. Bissinger gives us a chilling picture of how high school football in Odessa, Texas, mirrors many of the worst problems of professional sports. However, with all its problems, there is a Christian presence within organized sports that makes life in that community more interesting, dynamic, and meaningful than in many professional communities. This is because Christians made a deliberate strategic decision years ago to actively and effectively infiltrate that community with the salt of the Gospel.

More than in any other area of Ameri-can life, Christians are providing salt in almost every activity involving sports. The Fellowship of Christian Athletes provides a ministry for almost every high school and college in America. Athletes in Action provides a way for Christian athletes to use their athletic skills to win a hearing for the Gospel message. Every team in Major League Baseball, the National Football League, and the National Basketball Association has a chaplain who provides for everything from weekly chapel services to in-depth discipling of team members. Dave Dravecky, the courageous former major league pitcher who lost his arm to cancer, credits the discipling efforts of the baseball chaplains in San Diego and San Francisco with helping him to move toward maturity in Christ through systematic study of God's Word.

There is a Christian ministry devoted exclusively to the professional golf tour and one devoted exclusively to the professional tennis tour. Even the pro bass-fishing tour has chapel services.

There is almost no athletic gathering of any kind without a significant Christian component. The World Series, the Super Bowl, the Olympics, All-Star Games in all pro sports, major coaching conventions, and NCAA meetings all have prayer breakfasts, luncheons with Christian speakers, or special Bible studies. In addition, there is almost always a companion activity for, or outreach, to the wives.

Former Detroit sports writer Waddy Spoelstra edits an influential monthly publication called *Closer Walk* with the subtitle *The Christian Sports Insider.* The December 1991 edition carried this banner headline across the entire front page of the paper: "Superstar David Robinson Accepts Jesus Christ." The story describes how the seven-foot San Antonio Spurs center was led to Christ by the Spurs' chaplain. This paper is representative of sports' unself-conscious approach to the Gospel.

Most important, many well-known stars as well as movers and shakers in sports make their commitment to Christ very public. Such Hall of Fame caliber names as Tom Landry and Roger Staubach in football, Julius Irving in basketball, Orel Hershiser and radio announcer Ernie Harwell in baseball, and Stan Smith in tennis are only a representative few who openly and avidly proclaim Christ.

I do not mean to imply that the world of big-time sports is one great big Sunday school picnic. You and I both know it isn't. But it is an arena in which the Christian message is welcome, where individuals are not scorned because they believe in Jesus, and where some of the most highly respected leaders are known as much for their Christian commitment as for their athletic or managerial skill. Can you say that about the arena in which you work?

The reason why Christian faith is present in the sports community is that Christians did not run away the minute alcohol was served in a stadium, when games were played on Sunday, when gambling entered the picture. Instead, they reasoned that because some of these troubling elements were a part of sports, that was all the more reason for Christians to stay and add as much salt as possible.

And yet one of the first criticisms I overheard when I decided to go with the Miami Dolphins was "How can he be a Christian and work for an organization that promotes sports on Sunday?"

The contrast between sports and television can hardly be greater. In sports you meet Christians everywhere you go. In more than twenty years of working in television, I have met almost no openly confessing Christian working in mainstream television. The difference in the two communities can hardly be more pronounced. In sports, active Christians provide a life-enhancing seasoning just not present in television. Is it any wonder, then, that most of what is available on our home screens is so lacking in Judeo-Christian content? How can these television people be expected to accurately portray Christian values on the screen if there aren't any Christian producers, screenwriters, cameramen, or directors?

I went into the world of sports with very little encouragement from the church. I would venture to say there is even less encouragement within the church for someone to take his résumé to Burbank and interview for a job with

NBC. And we expect television to promote our values?

Let me take this opportunity to address some of the criticisms leveled at those who uphold the Christian presence in athletics. It goes something like this: with all the dynamic Christians involved, all the sports-related Christian ministries, and all the Christian influence at almost every level of sports, evil still exists and even grows. That's absolutely right, but as my friend Dr. Pritchard points out, "Salt retards spoilage. It doesn't prevent the process of decay, but it slows it down. . . ." I shudder to think about the condition of sports without Christian influence. Certainly there is still much that is wrong with sports, but I believe things would be worse if Christians had fled this arena. Our job as Christians is not to take over the various communities in our world; it is, however, to penetrate them, to be present, to provide God's alternatives to evil, to demonstrate Christ's relevance there, to be as good a representative as possible for Him and His church.

Too many Christians are more concerned about keeping score than being salt. The problem with this mindset is that we will not "win" in the way the world sees winning. Even if the church and its people do a very effective job of penetrating a particular community, as is the case with sports, evil will not be eliminated until our Lord returns and estab-lishes His new kingdom. Salt retards spoilage, it doesn't prevent it. It slows down decay, it doesn't stop it. Our responsibility is not to keep score but to keep living for Him. We know the ultimate victory will be ours through Christ. It will not, however, happen here. If we are effective, we will have many triumphs, many victories, many thrills as we see the Holy Spirit turn our efforts into positive benefits in the lives of some of those around us, but evil will survive, even prosper. We are called to be our best and to leave the results to Him.

The scorekeeping mentality is most pervasive in the way Christians approach television. The well-meaning Christian people working so ineffectively to improve television in America spend much of their time monitoring telecasts so they can tell us how many acts of violence, how many sexually explicit scenes, how many anti-Christian plots are seen on the nation's networks. Again, it seems to me, that our job is not so much to monitor evil as it is to provide alternatives to evil. If the resources used to survey all those hours of television, report those results, and then organize a boycott had been used to produce and distribute even one quality national program that pointed viewers to the more excellent way, that would be of more value than all the scorekeeping. And it would be much closer to fulfilling Christ's command to be salt in the world.

Sports teaches us another lesson about being salt, and it applies to all other fields of endeavor. We do not have to be the best to be effective, but we do have to be at our best.

Byron Ballard never progressed beyond the minor leagues as a baseball pitcher, but, because he was a solid, hard-working teammate, he won a hearing for the Gospel with Dave Dravecky while they were playing at Amarillo, Texas. Dave accepted Christ and went on to become an outstanding major league pitcher who was a powerful influence for good in the highest levels of baseball and continues to minister to many. Byron went for it. He used his skills and abilities to penetrate the professional baseball community, performed at his own personal peak, and after he had earned a hearing, effectively presented the Gospel message. Byron did not make it to the major leagues, but his influence did. Byron Ballard is the salt of the earth.

That's the kind of salt most of you reading this book can be. That's the kind of roaring lamb I'd like to see moving into every culture-shaping venue of our land.

Christians of both competence and commitment are needed to penetrate every area of society, and they need to do it with Christ's command to be salt firmly in mind. When the church sees only the professional ministry as a calling of concern, as a field of interest for the whole body, as a profession to be supported with prayer and financial support, kingdom building is terribly weakened.

How many churches have a strategy that seeks in very concrete measurable ways to equip its people to be salt every day and consciously targets areas of its community for penetration? Not nearly enough. This is much more difficult and requires much more thought than spending our time and effort promoting Sunday church attendance, special evangelism seminars, and a yearly missionary conference. Being a roaring lamb is not about special days, special emphases, special people, and special professions. Rather, it is about everyday people doing everyday jobs with a very special goal—that of effectively representing Christ in all areas of society. Our churches should exist for this.

At the very least, the young people of the church should be made to see that their careers, whatever they may be, are just as vital, just as much a concern of the congregation, and just as much a part of the mission of the church as are those of the foreign missionaries the church supports. This is in no way a call to support missionaries less, but does it seem right to have a budget for, sermon series about, and special emphasis on missionaries and to ignore the young people of the local congregation who will be heading into areas of life just as difficult and just as demanding as far as living out Christ's command to be salt and light is concerned as those entered into by any missionary?

Typically, the young people of a congregation who are called to the professional ministry are singled out for special attention, special counseling, special prayer, and special financial support. Why shouldn't talented young people of the congregation who hope to enter medicine, or teaching, or journalism, or writing, or plumbing, or retailing, or any other world of work be given at least the same kind of attention? At the very least, they should be made to understand that in their careers they have both the possibility and the responsibility to be a part of the ministry of the church. At the very least they should be instructed in the how of this as well as the why. Also, at the very least they should know that they are valued, being prayed for, and supported as they take the salt of the Gospel to their place of work every day. This is the way to make sure they become roaring lambs.

It is clear that the Scripture commands us to be salt in the world. It is clear that this demands penetration—not selective penetration but penetration of every area of society. It is clear that the command is to every Christian—not to some elite, professional class of Christians. It is clear that the way to be salt is to provide positive uplifting alternatives wherever we are as opposed to being negative and reactionary. It is clear that the call to be salt calls for both competence and commitment—we must be at our best in order to win the kind of hearing Christ deserves. It is clear that churches must consistently, consciously, and conscientiously provide an equipping ministry for the entire congregation, particularly for its young people, if Christ's command is to be carried out. It is clear that life anywhere without salt is bland and tasteless and is decaying at a faster rate than it should. It is clear that there is a price to be paid for being salt. The world will not always appreciate being stung by the salt of God's Word. It is clear that the command to be salt requires very little scorekeeping. Our responsibility is to do our best and to leave the results with Him in the knowledge that the ultimate victory is ours through Christ.

Finally, it is clear that the culture-shaping professions are especially salt-free. So the remainder of this book will take a closer look at some of those professions and challenge you to consider how you can be part of a mighty effort to reclaim those territories that we have given up.

The only way we can do that is to find some lambs who are willing to roar.

Conclusion

RICHARD BOLLES IS a seventy-three-year-old former Episcopal minister whose book, *What Color Is Your Parachute?*, perennially works its way to the top of the bestseller lists. Much of his life has been dedicated to helping folks navigate the complex issues that surround career and work.

Sitting in his home-office in a hillside community just outside of Oakland, Bolles explained that it's a mistake to attempt a "work for God" if it means letting your gifts lay by the wayside. "There is something wrong with the definition, if one ever comes to it, of saying, 'I'm doing this for God, but I hate it,'" he said.

Bolles, whose books have sold more than six million copies and been translated into ten languages over the last thirty years, starts each day by reading three newspapers. It was during this routine that he discovered a near-perfect example of his view of calling.

It wasn't a story about an entrepreneur whose company had taken him to the top. It wasn't a story about a hot CEO of an Internet company. And it wasn't a story about a star athlete. It was a story about a checker at a local Safeway supermarket.

The woman worked back in the days when cash registers had keys that were punched. There were no bar code readers to magically scan in the price of each item. "She would get a rhythm going on the keys of the cash register when she was ringing stuff up," Bolles told us. "Then she would challenge herself on how she packed the paper bag with the groceries."

When shoppers were unsure about how to cook what they were buying, she wrote out recipes for them. And, with permission from the parents who came through her line, she handed out candy to the kids.

As a job, it was work that just about anyone could have performed, "but she did it in her own unique way," said Bolles. "She performed all these different roles under the guise of 'just' being a checker. That's a basic way that calling gets or should get traced out: Taking mundane tasks and figuring out how to transfigure them.

"The story in the Gospels of Jesus going up on the mount and being transfigured before the disciples is to me a picture of what calling is all about. Taking the mundane, offering it to God, and asking Him to help us to transfigure it. It isn't a matter of doing a great work like bringing peace into the world necessarily; it may well mean being a checker. It's in the sense that there's a uniqueness to the way in which you do the task."

TAKING STOCK

As we said at the outset, this book is for people who want their work to be about something more than just putting bread on the table. It is for folks who want to discover and live out their callings in ways that honor God and maximize impact. For the great majority of us, that calling places us in a field that traditionally isn't considered "a ministry." Think about it for a second: In your community, how many people work in careers that most of us would describe as "ministry"? And how many work in careers that traditionally aren't considered "ministry"? Finally, how many people would tell you that their work—regardless of how it might be stereotyped by others—is their "ministry"?

As the chapters in this book illustrate, followers of Christ don't need to–and, in fact, shouldn't—segment life so that their faith has nothing to do with their work. It is essential, a Biblical mandate, for followers of Christ to integrate—to take advantage of the wisdom of the Scriptures and the guidance of the Holy Spirit to bring eternal significance to work.

The pages of this book provided some wonderful practical advice on how to get started. One of the advantages of a number of different content providers is that we gain a global perspective from many different vantage points. But one of the downsides can be an "all over the place" feeling that lacks uniformity or continuity. To guard against that sense of fragmentation, we have created a series of statements that attempt to bring all the content together in an overarching way.

Going beyond merely reiterating the messages of each chapter, these statements tie the thinking of the authors together. They fall under four headings: the purpose of work, the urgency of calling, the importance of clarity, and the value of difference.

The Purpose of Work

- Work is a good institution made by God that comes to us as both a privilege and a mandate.
- Work was designed by God to satisfy a rich multitude of life's needs in addition to economic necessities.
- The opportunities, disciplines, and pressures of the marketplace play a primary role in our continuous learning, growth, and maturity in Christ.
- Lessons learned in the crucible of the marketplace are frequently transferable to other parts of life.

The Urgency of Calling

- A personal and specific understanding of the call of Christ in our lives is absolutely essential but is often very difficult to know.
- If we are doing what He calls us to, then our work is His work and our career contributes to His eternal agenda.
- There is an important link between calling and a healthy work ethic.
- Periodic times of career evaluation that include the possibility of career adjustment contribute to work satisfaction and life impact.

The Importance of Clarity

- Any system of ranking between different kinds of work, including division between what is termed *sacred* and *secular*, is a human invention and completely contrary to Scripture.
- Scripture establishes the criterion upon which to build a successful work life, but a significant tension regularly exists between what God asks and what the professional environment demands.

The Value of Difference

- Our mandate to be salt and light might mean working in professions that are shunned by many followers of Christ.
- The art of leadership explained and illustrated in Scripture looks different than human models, including a principle mandate to make a significant difference in the lives of those being led.
- A life of workplace faith ought to yield vision that pushes us beyond mediocrity and an internal attitude that sets us apart as leaders.

TAKING ACTION

So where do we go from here? We would like to leave you with some action points that are based on the five sections of the book.

THE FOUNDATIONS: *Build your life at work on a personal relationship with Jesus.*

Ken Blanchard had established himself as a world-class speaker, writer, and teacher in the area of business management, and that's what had him puzzled. He stood at the top of the mountain and somehow wondered how he had gotten up the hill. Was he really *that* good?

He simply couldn't shake the feeling that some greater power was playing a role in his success. And the more he thought about it, the more he began to ask questions. And those questions eventually led him to answers that are found only in Christ. Through the leading of such friends as Bob Buford, Bill Hybels, and Phil Hodges, Blanchard eventually agreed to sign on with what Hybels labeled "the three-man consulting team"— the Father who started it, the Son who lived it and the Holy Ghost who is the day-to-day operational manager.

Blanchard, who now uses the title "Chief Spiritual Officer" for Blanchard Training and Development, already had written or co-written such bestsellers as *The One-Minute Manager*. And he was in high demand as a motivational speaker. But it was only after he accepted Christ that he really experienced success in his work.

"One of the things I started to realize is that if all you focus on is earthly success, you've got no chance of getting spiritual significance," Blanchard told us. "If, however, you focus on spiritual significance, you've got a chance of earthly success."

THE HURDLES: *Don't give in when a life of integrity is difficult or when the motivation to work hard goes away.*

As a tax attorney for a large corporation, Larry Langdon discovered that a vice president in the company was about to execute an illegal sale. "If you go through with this," Langdon bluntly told the man, "I'll ensure that you go to jail."

"He didn't appreciate that news," Langdon later said in an interview with *The*

Life@Work Journal. But when Langdon eventually left the company, that same man expressed his sincere appreciation for the stance he had taken.

"A walk of integrity has an initial cost," Langdon said. "But ultimately, people see the wisdom of doing things the right way."

There are many hurdles in the life of a follower of Christ in the marketplace, but most relate to the tension between what God wants and what the work environment is asking for. Sometimes, as Langdon pointed out, others eventually see the value of doing it God's way. Other times, they don't. But when viewed in light of eternity, doing right is never wrong.

THE TOOLS: *Spend a lifetime learning from Scripture and the myriad other resources available for professional development.*

When legendary theologian Harry Ironside began to lose his sight, two students agreed to work as his assistants. Among other things, they wrote out his correspondence and acted as his chauffeur. So if Ironside had a trip from Dallas to Tyler, Texas, as he often did, the students took turns driving him there and back.

One of those students was Howard Hendricks, and it was no accident that he wound up spending countless hours in a car with a genuine man of God who had comprehensive knowledge of Scripture. Hendricks, now a noted teacher, speaker, and theologian, was intentional in his quest to find mentors.

"I would figure out who the guy is who's got what I want, then ask, 'How can I get next to him, spend time with him?' " Hendricks said one day from his office at Dallas Theological Seminary.

Hendricks knew that there always were people who had traveled the road ahead of him, and it was up to him to go find them and learn from them.

TAKING THE LEAD: *Embrace any personal leadership challenge given by God and develop that gift toward maximum impact.*

Early in his political career, William Wilberforce made the decision to achieve two things, and any sensible person would have told him that neither was possible. One of his "great objectives" in life was to see the "reformation of manners" in England. The other was to see slavery abolished throughout the British Empire.

When it came to ending slavery, Wilberforce's challenge was so daunting that the preacher John Wesley told him it couldn't happen without a miracle. His words served as both a warning and as an encouragement. "Unless God has raised you up for this very thing, you will be worn out by the opposition of men and devils," Wesley wrote. "But if God be for you who can be against you?"

Wilberforce spent forty-seven years fighting this fight, and the final victory—which came only three days before he died in 1833—impacted not only the British Empire, but also Africa, India, and the United States. It literally changed the world.

And in a society where it was fashionable to be "loose in morals and skeptical in religion," as biographer John Pollock put it, Wilberforce played a critical role in making manners popular among his country's trendsetters. It changed the way business was conducted and it changed the government ruled.

"Whatever its faults," wrote Pollock, "nineteenth-century British public life became famous for its emphasis on character, morals, and justice and the British business world famous for integrity." (*A Man Who Changed His Times,* by John Pollock, The Trinity Forum Reading, Spring 1996)

The lesson: Never underestimate the influence of one Godly leader.

THE FUTURE: *Evaluate work opportunities and options against the current personal call of Jesus to determine what the career road map looks like from here.*

Raymond Lee looked at the sad state of America's inner cities, and his mind drifted halfway around the world to the poverty-stricken streets of India.

Urban areas of the United States overflowed with homeless people, yet he saw street after street after street of boarded-up buildings, each a monument to a once thriving downtown culture that now was fighting off rigor mortis.

"It's like going to Calcutta and seeing thousands of starving people while you see thousands of fat cows roaming around," Lee told us. "A lot of it is not a question of resources, but how you see the world and how you exercise stewardship. The right view of the world will lead to the right resource allocation."

So Lee and some friends founded Oasis Development Enterprises Inc., a for-profit real-estate development company that focuses on renovating rundown buildings while operating on overt Biblical principles.

"While we all are into investing to make strong financial returns, we also are interested in conscientious investing—finding the type of strategic investments that score well on both," he said. "This is making a handsome return and at the same time demonstrating the unity of the body of Christ."

Through this work, Lee and his teammates show Christ to investors, to high-ranking officials in city, state, and national governments, and to low-income citizens who benefit from well-run, low-cost housing that comes with the inner city renewal.

Lee was drawn by his faith in Christ to some critical needs. He saw some creative ways in which his skills and resources could help meet those needs. And, most importantly, he then acted on those needs.

TAKING NOTICE

As we've learned from the authors whose contributions appear in this book, a life at work yields multiple opportunities for discovery.

Discovering how God has gifted us, and how we fit in personally to His agenda for our generation. *Scripture labels that calling.*

Discovering how to make a difference as God's agent in our work context. *Scripture labels that leading.*

Discovering how to allow the Holy Spirit to work in our lives during the more than 100,000 hours we will spend in the marketplace over the span of our career. *Scripture labels that growth.*

Discovering how to respond to the hard and difficult things that any work environment will expose us to over time. *Scripture labels that perseverance.*

Discovering how to remain focused on Christ at work—on His power, His grace, His love, His security. *Scripture labels that worship.*

In one of his most popular songs, singer/songwriter Steven Curtis Chapman compared the Christian life to a great adventure. From calling and growth to perseverance and worship, our life at work is an exciting part of that great adventure.

From the truck driver to the CEO, from the farm hand to the president, from the homemaker to the pastor, God calls us all to blaze a trail for His glory.

Welcome to the adventure!

The editors of *The Life@Work Journal* wish to gratefully acknowledge the following publishers for the permission to reprint copyrighted materials.

Cook Communications Ministries for "Human Labor: Necessarily Evil or God's Design" from *Christians in the Marketplace* by Bill Hybels, copyright ©1992 by Cook Communications. Copied with permission. May not be further reproduced. All rights reserved.

NavPress for "Working for God—His Work, His Way, His Results" from *Your Work Matters to God*, copyright ©1987 by Doug Sherman and William Hendricks. Used by permission. All rights reserved.

The Free Press, a Division of Simon & Schuster, Inc., for "What Is a Calling?" from *Business as a Calling: Work and the Examined Life* by Michael Novak, copyright © 1996 by Michael Novak. Reprinted by permission.

Word Publishing for "Combating the Noonday Demon" from *The Call* by Os Guinness, copyright © 1998 by Os Guinness. For "Something's Not Working" from *Why America Doesn't Work* by Charles Colson and Jack Eckerd, copyright © 1991. And for "Vision: Seeing Beyond Mediocrity" from *Living Above the Level of Mediocrity* by Charles Swindoll, copyright © 1990.

Thomas Nelson Publishers for "Common Tensions Believers Face" from *Believers in Business* by Laura Nash, copyright © 1994. For "Basic Biblical Minimums" from *Business by the Book* by Larry Burkett, copyright © 1998. And for "The Extra Plus in Leadership: Attitude" from *Developing the Leader Within You* by John Maxwell, copyright © 1998.

Zondervan Publishing House for "Learning Is Everybody's Business" from *The Soul of the Firm* by William Pollard, copyright © 1996 by The ServiceMaster Foundation. Used by permission. For "Staying in the Game, but Adjusting the Plan" from *Halftime* by Bob Buford, copyright © 1994 by Robert P. Buford. Used by permission. And for "Salt: Make Use of It" from *Roaring Lambs* by Bob Briner, copyright © 1993 by Bob Briner. Used by permission.

Hyperion, an imprint of Buena Vista Books for "Introduction," The Selection Process," "He Did Not Kick the Donkey," and "He Said Why Not Me?" from *Jesus, CEO* by Laurie Beth Jones, copyright © 1995 by Laurie Beth Jones. Reprinted by permission.

Doubleday, a division of Random House, Inc., for "What Is Leadership?" from *Leadership Is an Art* by Max DePree, copyright © 1987 by Max DePree. Used by permission.

COMING SOON

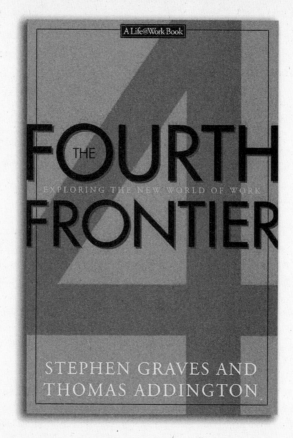

A Life@Work Book

THE
FOURTH
EXPLORING THE NEW WORLD OF WORK
FRONTIER

STEPHEN GRAVES AND
THOMAS ADDINGTON

Explore the new world of work—The Fourth Frontier

A new territory lies at the rim of the New Economy, a territory that has been around since the beginning of time but that is uncharted and foreign to most followers of Christ in the 21st century. It's the territory of work: the Fourth Frontier. Unlike other God-ordained institutions—church, family, and government—followers of Christ routinely treat work as a necessity; something we must do to make a living, a separate and discon-nected entity of existence. Addington and Graves show that work, in fact, is ordained by God. By exploring such landscapes as calling, devotion, stewardship, influence, integrity, and rest, readers can discover how to have a Kingdom influence in the marketplace while living an integrated life in the Fourth Frontier.

🔟 WORD PUBLISHING
www.wordpublishing.com